making matters

A Vocabulary for Collective Arts

Valiz

Contributors

Aliens in Green
a.pass / Lilia Mestre
Florian Cramer
Display Distribute / Elaine W. Ho
Feral Atlas / Lili Carr & Feifei Zhou
Anja Groten
Thalia Hoffman
Jatiwangi art Factory / Bunga Siagian & Ismal Muntaha
Eleni Kamma
Frans-Willem Korsten
Klaas Kuitenbrouwer
Pia Louwerens
Dani Ploeger
Kate Rich
Femke Snelting
Olu Taiwo
Janneke Wesseling
West / Baruch Gottlieb
West / Akiem Helmling
Z. Blace

Partners

Academy of Creative and Performing Arts, Leiden University
Het Nieuwe Instituut, Rotterdam
Waag, Amsterdam
West Den Haag
Willem de Kooning Academy and Piet Zwart Institute, Rotterdam

making matters

A Vocabulary for Collective Arts

Editors
Janneke Wesseling, Florian Cramer

Editorial committee
Florian Cramer, Anja Groten,
Klaas Kuitenbrouwer, Pia Louwerens,
Marie-José Sondeijker, Janneke Wesseling

Valiz

contents

⇸ making

↣ matter

⇝ undisciplined

making matters

a vocabulary for collective arts

Janneke Wesseling & Florian Cramer

The world today faces overwhelming ecological and social problems and the concern for material existence on earth is more pressing than ever. When looking at the field of art and design, this means that research into our relation to the world around us and the actual making of things has acquired a new urgency.[1] *Making Matters* asks what role visual artists and designers can play under these conditions. The book gathers a number of relevant making practices and investigates the urgency from which they arise.

One of the main departure points of *Making Matters* is the realization that collective action is necessary and inevitable, in society at large as well as in the field of the arts. Collective art and design practices therefore are the main focus of this book. They point to a transformation of working methods that not only shapes and changes practices but also affects artists and designers in their position and identity: from individuality and autonomy to experimental collectivity and collaboration; locally as well as globally.

A new perspective on 'making' becomes apparent here. When practices shift towards collaborative making processes instead of individual products, what does 'making' and the production of concrete, material 'things' mean? Artists collaborate with non-artists and in doing so may take on other identities, such as researcher, community activist, computer hacker, or business↦ consultant. The research done by these artists departs from the most diverse areas, from logistics↣ and biotechnology to geology or dance. As a result, the distinction between art, design, research, and activism is dissolving. It follows that these practices may hardly be recognizable as art

1. The term 'art' is used here in its broadest sense, encompassing visual art, design, performance art, new media practices and other artistic disciplines.

or design practices any longer, nor are their outcomes necessarily identifiable as artistic outcomes, let alone as specific art works. Some of these practices no longer conform to a conventional Western idea of art and art making. This book aims to identify some of their key concepts and to make their vocabularies accessible to a larger public.

The practices brought together in this book address specific ecological and social problems, sometimes explicitly, sometimes implicitly. All of them embrace the complexity of the various crises that we find ourselves in and try to develop ways of dealing with them. They experiment with and embody examples of new ways of living together and of a sustainable existence on Earth with all living beings.

Material artistic practices↣, i.e., ways of concrete making and doing, often go hand-in-hand with a theoretical inquiry. The textual and visual contributions in this book embody this intertwinement of conceptual and material thinking. The authors share an interest in artistic research↬, a relatively newly institutionalized research field that connects doing and thinking, making and theorizing, in a reciprocal exchange that does not prioritize one over the other. In artistic research↬, practical action (making) and theoretical reflection (thinking) go together, action and thought are inextricably linked.

Art contests the age-old dichotomy of theory and practice. Since Modernism, it has involved a constant questioning of the role of art and artist. The practices presented in this book put these questions on the table once more. They exemplify the attempt to bridge the distance between theory and practice, or even (in some cases) to obliterate the distinction between art production, critical reflection, and everyday life.

The roles of artist, curator, institution⊕→ (museum, Kunsthalle, artist-run spaces, biennial, documenta) and audience may become fused in the production of art.

This development raises fundamental questions of authorship and of the status quo of the art object and process: where is it situated and how can it be perceived or experienced? The materialization of art, its aesthetic dimension, its 'aesthetic—felt, spatio-temporal—dimension',[2] is acquiring new meaning and importance. In the light of the pressing challenges that we are facing on a global scale, and in the light of the critical and discursive potential of contemporary art practice, 'making' matters more than ever before.

how, on what ground, have the contributions to this book been selected?

Artists collectives are at the centre of attention in contemporary art discourse.[3] The 15th edition of the world's leading contemporary art exhibition documenta (2022) will bring the contemporary art phenomenon of multidisciplinary collectives to a wider audience. Not only are its curators, the Indonesian ruangrupa collective, such a collective themselves; most artists invited to documenta 15 are multidisciplinary collectives, too.

This book aims to contribute to the growing body of literature on the phenomenon of the art collective in its present-day, multidisciplinary, and hybrid form. It aims to provide insight into the subject matter of

2. Peter Osborne, *Anywhere of Not at All: Philosophy of Contemporary Art* (London and New York: Verso, 2013), p. 48.
3. For the 2021 Turner Prize only artist collectives were nominated: Array Collective, Black Obsidian Sound System, Cooking Sections, Gentle/Radical and Project Art Works.

these collective multidisciplinary practices. Most contributors are practitioners whose work falls in the cracks between the disciplines of art, design, critical theory, research, performance, community organization, social activism, and critical engagement with technology. Even when their work is grounded↣ in one of those disciplines, it usually encompasses at least two others. In the end, these practices and the texts in this book complicate the following questions: What is research when it is done by artists? What is 'making' when it is informed by critical theory and turned into activism? What is 'technology' when it is articulated by performance artists and in community projects? What happens when their implicit concepts, definitions, and vocabularies, which differ from mainstream understandings of those same concepts, are explicated in a specific vocabulary?

The project began with a four-year research project by our material practices↣ workgroup into the possibility of a crossover between art, design, and technology as an alternative to the capitalist-driven concept of the 'creative industries' consortium. It ended with the observation that alternative crossovers exist in the often overlooked and often overlapping fields of artistic research↬, artists' and designers' experiments with commons, Open Source culture, post-humanism and biopolitics, alternative economies, and community organization. Artists do not simply depict or reflect upon these varying perspectives from a critical distance, but radically translate them into their everyday ways of living and working, in other words, into material practices↣. This book aims to explicate tacit knowledge from artists' material practices↣ and from real-life experiments conducted in a world in crisis while gaining insight into present-day paradigm shifts in the arts.

The different disciplinary groundings of our contributors correspond to the respective disciplinary groundings and research specializations within the material practices↣ workgroup: Leiden University, Willem de Kooning Academy, Het Nieuwe Instituut, Waag, West Den Haag. Based on the expertise and the discussions in the workgroup, contributors were invited who could help to both focus and complicate the question of how artists practices and real-life experiments amount to knowledge for ways of living and survival in the planetary crisis.

reading guide

The vocabulary of concepts relating to collective material art practices↣ presented here is not an encyclopaedia nor even an inventory and it is by no means complete. It may be regarded as a thought experiment, aimed at stimulating further debate and new vocabularies.

The entries are categorized under seven headings, laid out in alphabetical order: bodies, collective, critique, economy, making, matter, and undisciplined. In some cases, entries refer to connected entries. The order of reading is not linear. You are invited to read the entries in any given order.

bodies

--->

collective bodies

Klaas Kuitenbrouwer

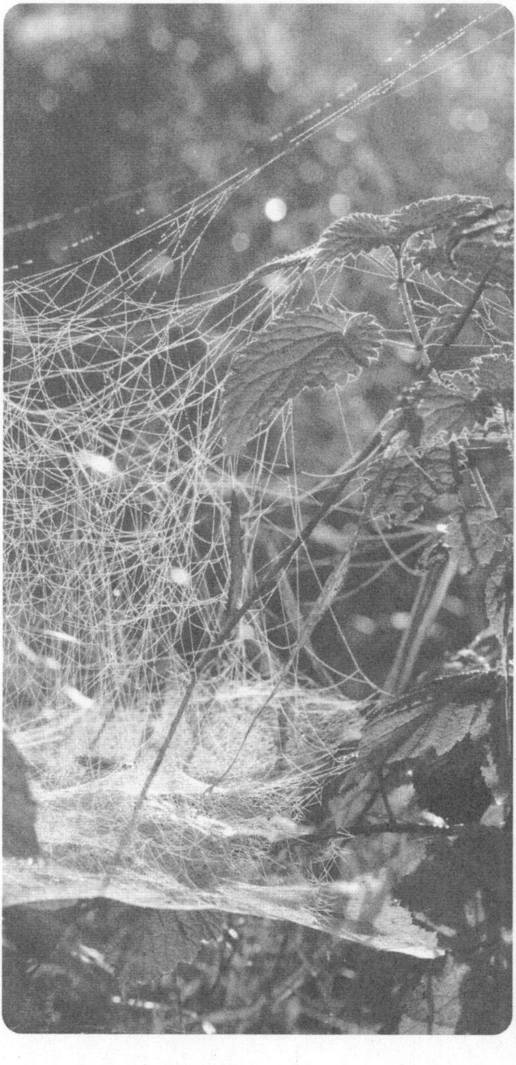

Photo: Patricia de Ruijter – mediakaal.nl.

--->

Starting a Zoöp⇛ is to declare a new *collective body.* It is laying out a new, shared skin. This is the first act in zoönomy↦, a practice of fostering ecological integrity for groups consisting of radically different, human, and other-than-human bodies that find themselves joined together in this new type of community.

A Zoöp⇛ is an effort to claim a shared reality among highly divergent bodies. To call them a collective body is partly a trick, a move to direct attention. It is partly hopeful aspiration and partly something that was found to be part of the idea of 'body' all along.

Zoöps⇛ consist of wide varieties of bodies: other-than-human bodies such as microbes and earthworms, trees, plants and algae, water bodies and more; human artefacts such as buildings, machines, and such; organizational bodies such as teams, boards, associations; legal bodies such as owners, third parties with contracts, municipalities, jurisdictions. Clearly, all these bodies are by themselves collective bodies, too, even when they nominally join the Zoöp⇛ as single entities.

To start a Zoöp⇛ is thus to articulate a new collective body by saying: you now belong together in a new way. This is the trick. This collection of collective bodies now has to find out how to live together. That is the aspiration.

Any non-abstract, materially existing body is not a singular thing anyway. A singular point only exists as a mathematical construct and abstraction. Any actual dot in any world is never a point but a body and, by that virtue, also some kind of multiplicity—it has an outside and therefore an inside.

All collective bodies are networks and part of networks, connected to myriads of other bodies. Many bodies are members of multiple collectives at the same time. Therefore, the boundary of any collective body is not fixed. A collective body's shared skin needs to be enacted, performed,[1] for a specific purpose and context, and once it has been recognized (or resampled symbolically) by other collective bodies, it will be more sharply defined. It will shimmer into place. New bodies join all the time, and some bodies leave. Performing such a shared skin is the ongoing effort of every Zoöp⇛.

To do the work of the skin is to metabolize particularities of the world and also to put up some resistance—on behalf of the body—to being metabolized. A degree of metabolization is necessary for a body to exist, to be present, but to be metabolized entirely is to cease to exist.[2]

The constituents of a collective body remain intact bodies. They still have their own skins—a bit thinner at some places, maybe.

The Umwelt or life-world[3] of any body is that which can be metabolized: chemically, aesthetically, conceptually, politically, economically. Different bodies, different rules, different chemistry.

1. Karen Barad, *Meeting the Universe Halfway: Quantum Physics and the Entanglement of Matter and Meaning* (Durham, NC: Duke University Press, 2007).
2. Extrapolated from Elizabeth Povinelli, *Geontologies: A Requiem to Late Liberalism* (Durham, NC: Duke University Press, 2016).
3. Jakob von Uexküll, *A Foray into the Worlds of Animals and Humans: With a Theory of Meaning* (Minneapolis: University of Minnesota Press, 2010), originally published in German: *Streifzüge durch die Umwelten von Tieren und Menschen* (Berlijn: Verlag von Julius Springer, 1934).

---→

embeddedness

Pia Louwerens

My name is Pia Louwerens. You may be surprised to read a text written in the first person in a lexicon of collective material practices↣, but I would like to ask you to read my I, myself, as a collective effort in and by itself. Without you I wouldn't be here after all. And whatever I have done, as a 'junior embedded artistic researcher', I didn't come up with that myself. I held the job of junior embedded artistic researcher at the research project that this lexicon is part of. I decided that my research, asking how the artist performs within the institution⊕›, had to start with this peculiar job description.

In this case, the word *embeddedness*⇢ has an institutional provenance. The governmental organs who funded this research project are tailored to academic research in which this term indicates a specific institutional relationship. You can imagine a research project in the field of biology, in which case a junior researcher would do their research at one of the commercial partners of the project (the laboratory of a company, for example). They would, as a result, be 'embedded' in that company.

When you replace the biologist with an artist, you can see how this description inadvertently sketches out an unusual practice, reminiscent of the placement of artists in non-art organizations by the Artist Placement Group in the 1970s and 1980s. On top of that, I was placed or embedded in an exhibition space, which already works with artists, but in different capacities. They exhibit artists, and the staff is also populated by many young artists. I would be embedded as an artist in an institution⊕›, but not working at the institution⊕› as an artist; it would be different. How, I didn't know yet.

Online searches for embeddedness⇢ quickly lead to a specific context: it denotes the position of journalists who travel with the military to report from the front

--→

lines. I can't think of a more paranoid image.[1] In addition to these two perspectives, I also like to think of the more basic reading of embeddedness--→: two objects of different materials, one big and one small, where the smaller object is firmly lodged inside the other. I imagine a stone in a riverbed, creating an impression with its shape, while it gets smoothed over time.

My adoption of the condition of embeddedness--→ as a research subject, was precisely the start of my performance of embeddedness--→. Because of certain misconceptions that originated in modernity, artists are not encouraged to embed or lodge themselves firmly in their own conditions. This relates to causality: as an autonomous artist, the primary cause for action should be your own initiative (inspiration, or creation). Artists, like artworks, like art in general, strive to be free and independent, separate. To explain the misconception I think of a Spinoza Symposium at the contemporary art space West Den Haag, where I first heard Spinoza's parable of the stone that was thrown.[2] If the stone, Spinoza wrote, would get a consciousness mid-air, it would mistake itself into thinking that it made itself fly. If the artist is a stone, then 'the institution-⊕→' (see institution as practice-⊕→) controls most of the conditions that make it fly and keep it flying.

When considering the embedded state of a stone, we might observe its conditional dependence, but we can only do so by grace of its difference. There is by definition a difference between the stone and the

1. Eve Kosofsky Sedgwick, 'Paranoid Reading and Reparative Reading, or, You're So Paranoid, You Probably Think This Essay Is About You', in *Touching Feeling* (Durham and London: Duke University Press, 2003), pp. 123–152.
2. Moira Gatens, 'Living on the Gallows?', Spinoza & the Arts Symposium (West Den Haag), 4 October 2019.

riverbed, between object A and object B. If they were the same, there would be no embeddedness⇢ to observe. To get back to this particular project: if I, as an artist, use the infrastructure of the institution⇢ in the same way as other artists, I would not be embedded anymore. Or, if you insist that all artists are in embedded relation to the institution⇢, I can point out that I wasn't only embedded in the institution⇢, but in the institutional position of embeddedness⇢ as well.

Something that helped me think through the tension between embeddedness⇢ and difference is the figure of the parasite. As A.M. Gullestad wrote: 'Parasites are both a part and not a part of the host's body, neither self nor non-self.'[3] They exist in relation, yet do not assimilate. Through time, the strangeness of the parasite might be appropriated by the host. This phenomenon is deeply ingrained in our bodies: the mitochondria that energize our cells are said to have started out as parasites, they even have their own DNA.[4] Gullestad links the notion of parasite to the notion of 'minor literature' which Deleuze coined in a book on Kafka, a writer who lived and worked in Prague as part of a German-speaking minority: 'To Deleuze, minor literature is therefore not external, but internal to a major language, yet at the same time "foreign" to it.'[5] This sounds a lot like embeddedness⇢. Thinking through the parasitic, embeddedness⇢ evokes paranoia: who is using whom? Am I using the energy that the mitochondria provide, or is it the mitochondria 'who walk through the local park in the morning... thinking my thoughts?'[6]

3. Anders M. Gullestad, 'Literature and the Parasite', *Deleuze Studies* 5, no. 3 (2012), p. 314, doi.org/10.3366/dls.2011.0023.
4. Lewis Thomas, *The Lives of a Cell* (Toronto, New York and London: Bantam Books, 1974), p. 2.
5. Gullestad, 'Literature and the Parasite', p. 312.
6. Thomas, *The Lives of a Cell*, p. 3.

--→

This parasite/host relationship is not clear-cut. Just like we have parasites fuelling our cells, we have bacteria in our intestines, digesting our food; strangers truly are inside of us. I can fantasize about being external to the infrastructure of art, for example, but we, as artists, makers, readers of this lexicon, are the bodies through which the institution-⊕→ of art propagates. I host the institution-⊕→, as much as I am a parasite.

Before despairing—because how does one research something one is so much entangled with?—I tell myself that there might be no true distance, no separability to hold on to, but there is no true proximity either (see criticality-⊕→). I am a different material, I practice differently. Following the model of embeddedness--→ does not have to lead me to assimilation. The main questions I ask myself are: Which shape does the institution-⊕→ that is *embedded* in me imprint on my practice, and which shape do I imprint on the institution--→ as an embedded artistic researcher? How am I hosted and how do I host?

--->

embeddedness

Femke Snelting

Embeddedness⇢: a triple d word with tentacles in geology, surfacing every trouble possible from dependency to duress. There is nothing simple about this term: embeddedness⇢ means to be attentive to multiple inter-operating spacetimes, to resonate with what is below as well as with what is above and *delà*, to resist extraction, and to account for remote implications.[1]

> In assembling ideas that are seemingly disconnected and uneven (the seabird and the epilogue, the song and the soil, the punch clock and the ecosystem, the streetlight and the kick-on-beat), the logic of knowing-to-prove is unsustainable because incongruity appears to be offering atypical thinking. Yet curiosity thrives.[2]

embeddedness⇢:
to be set solidly into a mass

Ship merchants operating from the Liverpool docks in the nineteenth century needed the tides predicted and their clocks calibrated, so they commissioned the Bidston Observatory. The observatory was to be

1. This contribution is based on the script for a performative introduction to the sub-vault of the Bidston Observatory Artistic Research Centre (BOARC) for participants of the work session Down Dwars Delà, organized by Constant and BOARC, Liverpool, August 2021, constantvzw.org/site/Open-call-study-session-Down-Dwars-Dela-2-UK.
2. Katherine McKitttrick, *Dear Science and Other Stories* (Durham: Duke University Press, 2021), p. 4.

strategically situated on the highest point of the Wirral peninsula, overlooking the river Mersey, the river Dee, and the Irish sea. Completed in 1866, it was made out of sandstone extracted from the bedrock below, creating a cavity which now forms the observatories' extensive basements.[3] Around the building, a deep moat was dug to minimize interference from neighbouring traffic. The plinth in the picture (p. 30) is a 'bedrock connection point', located in the observatory sub-vault. Sheltered from temperature shifts and movements from elsewhere, the plinth provided a stable platform⇛ for a century of exacting earth observation.

Cornwall, last fall. Suddenly they feel the ground tremble, and hear windows rattle. Afterwards, Dr. Ryan Law, managing director of Geothermal Engineering explains to the local press:

> As part of the United Downs Deep Geothermal Power testing, we did cause some micro-seismicity. Although this was within our regulatory limits, we are stopping operations until we understand the cause. The tremors are low-scale and should not be anything to be afraid of.[4]

3. The Bidston Observatory was built on the solid bedrock of the Wirral peninsula, 'a capping of Keuper sandstone on soft Upper Bunter', which was considered to be more stable than other geological arrangements elsewhere. Joyce Scoffield, *Bidston Observatory: The Place and the People* (Merseyside: Countyvise Ltd, 2006).
4. Sabi Phagura, 'Houses shake as Cornwall is rocked by FIFTEEN "earthquakes" measuring up to 1.5 in magnitude in two days caused by tests at geothermal drilling site', *Daily Mail*, 1 October 2020, dailymail.co.uk/news/article-8794885/Houses-shake-Cornwall-rocked-15-earthquakes-two-days.html.

Geothermal energy is produced by harnessing heat from the earth's core. To produce power from this heat, extremely deep wells need to be drilled and water is pumped through them at high pressure. Since the Bronze age, Cornwall has been mined for tin, copper, arsenic, and lithium. Tremors in the porous underground are set off as a result of the additional disturbance caused by geothermal boring. In the non-committal words of the general manager, they sense all the troubles that wreck the earth: 'we caused micro-seismicity' ... 'within our regulatory limits' ... 'until we understand the cause' ... 'not anything to be afraid of'.

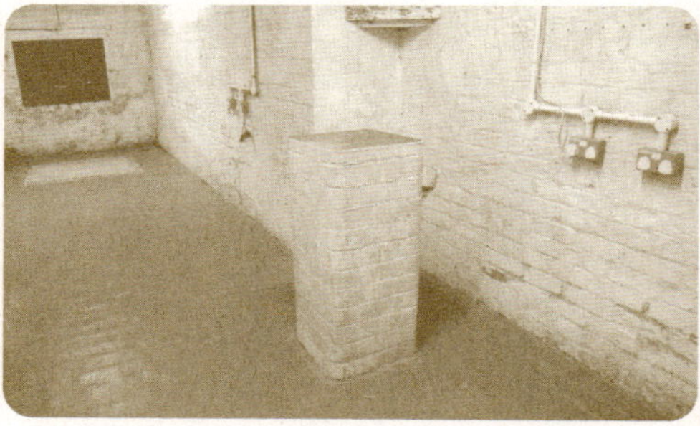

© Kym Ward (2022).

embeddedness→: laying in a bed of surrounding matter

South or north of here, already more than ten years ago. It takes him many long days to level the driveway of his holiday home. Using a *barre à mine*, a forged iron bar originally used by miners to pound the ground and break the surface, his movements reverberate through the valley. Eventually, he hits an immovable piece of rock and the pounding stops. He points, almost proudly, and says: 'look, the earth!'

Early on, the observatory installed a seismometer on the sub-vault plinth. Kept in the dark, it continuously auto-registered slight movements on light sensitive paper that corresponded with earthquakes experienced on the other side of the planet. A Milne-Shaw Vertical Tiltmeter was acquired in 1910, a precision instrument based on the same principle as the seismograph, where one part remains stationary and fixed, while another part moves together with the earth's surface. The vertical tiltmeter derives its precision from using a rigid arm that points upwards, with a pendulum hanging down from it. The swinging of the pendulum, with its fulcrum fixed to the bedrock connection point, makes micro-seismicity observable by magnifying the actual motion of the earth. It was with this instrument that the phenomena of 'tidal load' could be observed, the oscillating north-south tilt of the Wirral peninsula due to the strain of the water weighing down the bedrock (and subsequently, the plinth itself) at high tide.

A physiotherapist once told me about her interest in how bodies feel their way around with the help of instruments. She explained her fascination through the example of cooking a soup or a sauce. If you stir the bottom with a wooden spoon, she said, you will feel precisely at which moment it starts to catch. You do not need to put your hand into the hot liquid to touch the bottom of the pan.

At the observatory, the so-called 'ocean loading effect' continued to be registered with increased precision until the early seventies, when the expanding data about earth tides from around the world started to show unexplained discrepancies in neighbouring sites: the magnitude of the north-south tilt varied by twenty percent when measured in one end of its sub-vault, or the other. In an article called 'Tidal Tilt Anomalies', two scientists working at Bidston claimed that these inconsistencies could be explained by unknowable couplings between the landmass movement and the strain on the site itself. 'A mine or a tunnel, in which tilt measurements are usually taken, represents a discontinuity in the Earth's crust.'[5] By comparing different types of instruments, they found that tiltmeters were extremely accurate but that they were measuring tidal tilt in combination with hyper local movements due to situated geological conditions. Tidal tilt observations where eventually abandoned due to non-compliant embedded data.

embeddedness⇢: trembling with the earth

As with many material evidences of techno-scientific progress, the appointing of stability, the fixing of a point zero wherever convenient, seems to require an entitled mode of being in the world.

> Each point is merely a conceptual marker, which can be assigned and reassigned in the equation hierarchy as the ‹coordinating zero point› and every line can be formed to be the ‹coordinating axis›.[6]

Power arranges itself around such arbitrary vantage points, through which the movement of goods and people elsewhere can be controlled. Contributing to the reliable navigation of ships across the British

5. T.F. Baker and G.W. Lennon, 'Tidal Tilt Anomalies', *Nature* 243 (1973), pp. 75–76.
6. Clancy Wilmott, *Mobile Mapping Space: Cartography and the Digital* (Amsterdam: Amsterdam University Press, 2020).

--->

empire, but also actively and continuously supporting the convenient fable of transparent observation, the Bidston Observatory aligned with different scales of capitalist endeavour, exploitation, colonialist and imperialist modes of worlding.[7]

He is being driven around his native island Martinique, pointing out the places that he grew up in and that vanished after the earthquakes. The island is part of an archipelago located on the crumbling intersection of two tectonic plates, which makes the geo-plasticity of the earth regularly interact with human activity. 'We understand the world better if we tremble with it', he explains.[8]

To be embedded depends politically nor epistemologically on a fixed locus of observation. It opposes systematic thinking without fear, because it is a mode of understanding the world that resonates with the multidimensional and multidirectional impact of being embedded, of its inherent instability. Embeddedness---> is to 'tremble with the world'.

The image cuts back to the view from the car window, an undulating green landscape moving by under a bright blue sky filled with clouds. He continues:

> The world trembles in every way. It trembles organically and geologically. It trembles even with the climate, poor me, as far as I know. But the world also trembles through the relations we have with each other.[9]

7. 'The Center is Open/HECS is ajar!', wiki.bidstonobservatory.org/index.php/About.
8. Manthia Diawara, 'One World in Relation: Édouard Glissant in Conversation with Manthia Diawara', *NKA Journal of Contemporary African Art* 28 (Spring 2011), pp. 4–19.
9. Ibid.

gestures

Baruch Gottlieb

Czechoslovakian philosopher of communication Vilém Flusser asserted that the written word, with its linear, causal form of argumentation, was no longer sufficient to grapple with a world of technical effects occurring globally at the speed of light. One of his prescient claims was that what he called 'technical images' would take cultural precedence over the foregoing dominance of text. He defined technical, or synthetic images, as 'projections from the level of code', code inscribed in the apparatuses of modernity, be these technical or institutional. Technical images are, according to Flusser, 'images of texts' and thus synthesize human knowledge in forms that speed up critical responsiveness such that it can keep up with a very unstable condition.

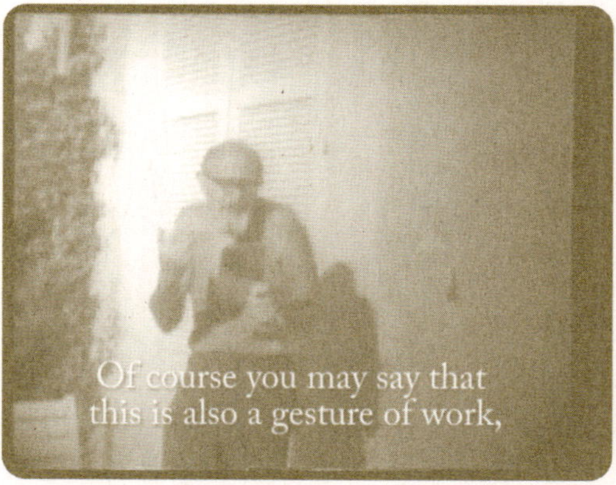

Fred Forest, *Les Gestes du Professeur*, U-matic video, B/W, 1974.

But what would those technical images look like? How might they come to be employed for the critical purpose proposed by Flusser? Luckily, he was able to demonstrate what he had in mind, in a series of collaborations with artists. In experimental videos that he made with the sociological artist Fred Forest,

Flusser explored the power of the human *gesture* as one of the new possibilities for critical human thinking, unlocked through video technology. In the video, Flusser can be seen gesturing avidly as he speaks about gesture. Forest, too, is instructed to gesture with his camera movements, and to criticize Flusser through these gestures. Likewise, Flusser instructs the future viewers of the video to use their own gestures in order to criticize both him and Forest. The viewers' gestural feedback should then, Flusser and Forest intended, be captured on video, too, and edited into the next iteration of the tape.

This playful exercise is not only a new form of philosophy for the age of technical images. It also points to a more general critique of cultural production. The semantic content of an utterance fades behind the gesture with which the utterance is made. Additionally, this thinking through gestures is patently embodied and situated: It breaks with the enlightenment and modern-age pretension of an abstract, disembodied, pure rationality, embraces contingency, subjective experience, and becomes open for more people. Flusser's commitment was in tune with his times and various critical revisions of enlightenment rationality in the twentieth century. It was an answer to the challenge of how to reject disembodied rationalism without also giving up the possibility of critical thinking. This issue had also been explored by his contemporaries Marshall McLuhan —with his penchant for slang and vernacular— and Donna Haraway with her leaky neologisms and troubled ironies.

In the gesture, the intent of the utterance and the effects it produces, the experience it generates, is more important than any particular semantic content. In other words, non-verbal communication is more important than verbal communication, connotation more important than denotation. Consider the Facebook algorithm, which allows advertisers to manipulate the emotions of target demographics in real time, as revealed in the 2017 Cambridge Analytica scandal. Advertisers no longer send merely one message lauding their product. Instead, they send a series of messages, which in their aggregation nudge their human targets towards the desired purchases or other behaviour. In the electronic age, the gesture of publishing is thus fragmented into myriad probing moments. As McLuhan quipped, the medium is the massage.

A show in the cybernetic community⇛ Alphabetum, 'Free Emojis', explored emojis as a contemporary manifestation of gestural communication. What Flusser had provoked his readers with in the 1980s, has become today's reality. Digital natives are indeed finding that technical images are far more apt for the analysis, commentary, and communication of our experience in the electronic age. Conversely, by observing emoji use we discover that text has not disappeared. In fact, we are writing and reading more than ever before while text has become more explicitly gestural.

--→

hosting

Eleni Kamma

Hosting: a material practice↣ that is linked to events in which humans are invited to participate. Hosting as a material practice↣ relates to conditions of production in the field of socially engaged art, aimed at creating a community. Hosting operates in hybrid contexts between the physical and the online. Its relevance for social, technological, and cultural interactions is the re-imagination of how 'I' may relate to 'we' and vice versa.

During the Making Matters conference (November 2020), three live Etherpad sessions were hosted by researchers Anja Groten, Eleni Kamma and Pia Louwerens. These were interactive meetings in an online collaborative notepad, where participants discussed symposium topics that came up during the conference. Each of the three sessions experimented with online collaborative engagement. Communicating through the pad takes place purely on a level of ideas and writing and utilizes one's ability to relate mentally through typing. All participants control and co-edit the text that is produced on the pad during the meeting. Despite its democratic intentions, the pad privileges those who prefer writing over speaking as a means of expression; it does not allow for equal access or experience for analphabets, people who have dyslexia and other learning disorders; and it excludes active participation for those not explicitly invited to the conversation. The one(s) who set up a conversation on the pad are also those who establish the group and do the inviting by sending the link. It depends on the pad's host(s) whether they will publicly or privately share the link online.

On March 3, 2021, I explored 'hosting' further through an online participatory event hosted by Jubilee, a platform⇛ for artistic research⇸ and production, of which I am a member. The aim of this experimental public event, which consisted of four unique presentations, was to offer perspectives on nourishing through online communication tools. Upon registration, future participants were sent four simple 'recipes' (each conceived by one of the event's hosts: Samah Hijawi, Philippine Hoegen, Eleni Kamma and Gosie Vervloessem), which they were invited to prepare beforehand. This event was recorded.

My prepared script went as follows:

1. Welcoming the audience (we see and hear each other on Zoom)

Welcome! Tonight, we will explore a pilot version of 'The Corners of the Mouth', a project I initiated that focuses on our current hybrid life of physical confinement and increased online presence. How can we use this hybridity to cultivate new forms of artistic expression and strengthen the relation between 'I' and 'we' ('we' meaning: virtual communities of contemporary online users)? Tonight, I, Eleni Kamma, have invited Brussels-based artists Samah Hijawi, Gosie Vervloessem and Philippine Hoegen to share their expertise in practicing affective communication. Over the following two hours, we will offer different perspectives on recipes and nourishment. First, I will take around 20–25 minutes and ask you to take your drink and join us on Etherpad. Please stop your videos but do not mute yourselves. The link is in the chat. Please follow it and meet me there.

2. Participants come to the pad (we hear each other on Zoom)

Please position your cursor in the space of the pad and experiment with typing. Could you share your name and what you are currently drinking with us?

I would encourage you to actively sense how your favourite beverage slowly slides from your mouth into your digestive system during the following twenty minutes.

During the first lockdown I became interested in whether Etherpad, an open-source online text editor, can reflect collectivity in these times. On Etherpad, each user's contributions are indicated by a colour code and recorded onscreen in real time. Thought processes are revealed as thinking takes shape through typing. The pad enables writing that is collectively performed and witnessed.

I type:

> 72 On the pad, the "I" and the "we" are simultaneously in common view.

Since then (especially during lockdowns), I think about communication under hybrid conditions, more precisely about possibilities to create affect by combining physical and digital communication processes.

--→

I type:

> · Can we consider our recent experiences of combined physical confinement and increased online presence as an opportunity to re-evaluate how we perceive relations between "I" and "we"?

Faced with this question, I consulted the *I Ching or The Book of Changes*, an ancient Chinese form of divination consisting of 64 hexagrams. With a question in mind, you drop the coin six times, receiving a hexagram. The answer to my question was:

> Hexagram 27 The Corners of The Mouth
>
> *The Image*
> *At the foot of the mountain, thunder:*
> *The image of Providing Nourishment. Thus, the superior man is careful of his words and temperate in eating and drinking.*
>
> *The Judgement*
> *The Corners of the Mouth. Perseverance brings good fortune. Pay heed to the providing of nourishment and to what a man seeks to fill his own mouth with.*

Several readings by commentators are available, such as Richard Wilhelm's:

> 116 This hexagram is a picture of an open mouth; above and below are firm lines of the lips, and between them the opening. Starting with the mouth, through which we take food for nourishment, the thought leads to nourishment itself. Nourishment of oneself, specifically of the body, is represented in the three lower lines, while the three upper lines represent nourishment and care of others, in a higher, spiritual sense.

I am puzzled about how to interpret this.

What abstract images can 'we' construct with the question, the people involved, the time and place we are in? I will now feed the pad with the Hexagram's lines that led me here. I invite you to a collaborative reading of the text. Let's eat and digest the Hexagram's words together. I invite you to vocalize the text, any way you like, loud, soft, or in your own language. Please try to both respect your rhythm and listen to the others!

— Line 1 (bottom line): You let your magic tortoise go, and look at me with the corners of your mouth drooping. Misfortune.
— Line 2: Turning to the summit for nourishment, deviating from the path to seek nourishment from the hill. Continuing to do this brings misfortune.
— Line 3: Turning away from nourishment. Perseverance brings misfortune. Do not act thus for ten years. Nothing serves to further.

--→

— Line 4: Turning to the summit for provision of nourishment brings good fortune. Spying about with sharp eyes like a tiger with insatiable craving. No blame.
— Line 5: Turning away from the path. To remain persevering brings good fortune. One should not cross the great water.
— Line 6 (top line): The source of nourishment. Awareness of danger brings good fortune. It furthers one to cross the great water.

While I am typing this, we hear an ensemble of voices reading/translating the text in several languages. Simultaneously, the user icons indicate who speaks on Zoom.

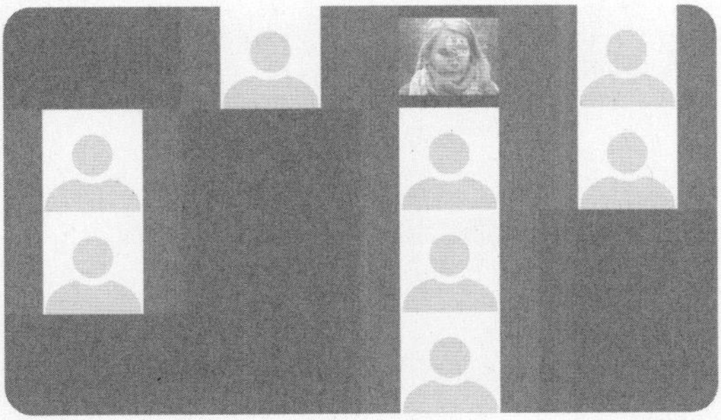

Thank you! Let's take five minutes together on the pad. Consider it a digestion-absorption process. Feel free to select a spot on the pad, to find your position along the text. You are welcome to re-feed the pad and the rest of us with your thoughts, feelings, experiences, and concerns in relation to 'The Corners of the Mouth'.

Audio playing: (belly noises) Water enters the hungry belly

Line 4

Turning to the summit for provision of nourishment brings good fortune. Spying about with sharp eyes like once someone asked my to think myself as an animal and I choose a tiger but it was a little one, totally unarmed. now the word tiger makes me think of my vulnerabilities. with insatiable craving.ever insatiable No blame.No shame.

I also wish I had sharp eyes like a tiger yes, sharp eyes, if only....laser sharp.

Line 5 I choose to me in the 5th line now.

Turning away from the etherpad. To remain persevering brings good fortune. One should not cross the great water, one should swim in it. Because that is where the fish is. and where the fish is, is happiness for there is silence and cold. Fish is thus happy.

Line 6 (top line)as we play, write, the words that we spoked vibrate in the body. their shapes COLORS not so much the meanings. that is lost or seems unimportant as the EVENT that hapen took the first place.

The source of nourishment. Awareness of danger brings good fortune. yet sometimes unawereness of danger also ironically brings good fortune. i agree It furthers (stranger thing: to go further towards crossing) one to cross the great water.(water_emotions) I feel my saliva gethering at the back of my throat.

[illegible] really seems a hangry belly

belly noises

Water enters the hungry belly...

the water was already there. Hunger merely made us aware of it

I feel my belly expanding

Are we all in one belly?

space harmony

Olu Taiwo

A choreological perspective offers an interesting starting point for understanding the return beat ⊕→. Choreology is the aesthetics and study of human movement through movement notation. Particularly Rudolf Laban's initial notions of 'effort' and 'place', as situated in the seat of sensation of the performer, and actioned in relation to the body's physical journal, give relevant entry points.

From his Rosicrucian roots, dancer and choreographer Rudolf Laban created a movement praxis he called choreutics, which reflected what he articulated as *space harmony*. It is based on patterns of rhythm and balance that can be perceived everywhere in nature, including in human anatomy. Laban saw spatial patterns in the pathways of human movement and recognized in these the shapes of the Platonic Solids. Expressive human movement closely aligned with the inclinations in the structure of these regular polyhedral forms.

Laban took the spatial patterns that follow the Platonic Solids as forms to be actualized through human movement. He came to articulate specific Movement Scales: a series of patterned movement sequences that performers can repeat; moving through these pathways in a predefined way. These Scales linked the natural spatial gestures→ of human bodies that move along all directions and inclinations to the directions of the vertices of a platonic shape. Following these movement Scales opens up the body in space and also enlarges spatial awareness. It balances the body spatially and aesthetically. This is why this spatial practice is called space harmony.

At the same time, Rudolf Laban further investigated the nature of harmonious and efficient effort and coined the term eukinetics to address this study. eukinetics is a combination of two Greek root words—'eu' meaning beautiful or harmonious and 'kinetikos' meaning movement. During the final two decades of his career in England, Laban's interest and analysis shifted from creative and artistic movement to a broader concern with human movement in general.

In parallel to this he dropped the exotic word eukinetics and adopted the more common English term, 'effort.' The term addresses an abstracted concept, that when studied always needs to be understood in context. How effort is situated can be seen by answering a number of key questions. Whose efforts are we referring to? What are the reasons for this effort? Where and when does the effort take place? How does the effort take place? Why is this effort performed at all? Working with these and other questions in his investigation of effort led Laban to identify two main domains of action, both of which give rise to practices of ever refining mastering of spatial experience and spatial skill. One group is comprised of goal-oriented actions such as sports⤳ and political and commercial endeavours. The attention of the bodies engaged in these actions is focused on the exterior and their spatial skills are applied to navigating and strategizing the use of space outside the body. The other group of actions is directed towards expressive goals such as artistic gestures⇢, religious and cultural performance. The attentions of bodies engaged in these kinds of actions is focused internally, and their skills are applied in charting an outward expression of their inscapes. This second group of actions also leads to and mobilizes self-knowledge.

Performing and experiencing the return beat⊕› provides the metaphysical context for both forms of effort, where both the navigated inscapes of the percipient practitioner, and their outward expressions of goal-oriented action are spatial, and the extra internal dimensions of self-awareness can lead to self-knowledge. As such, the return beat⊕› facilitates a wave-field for human activity.

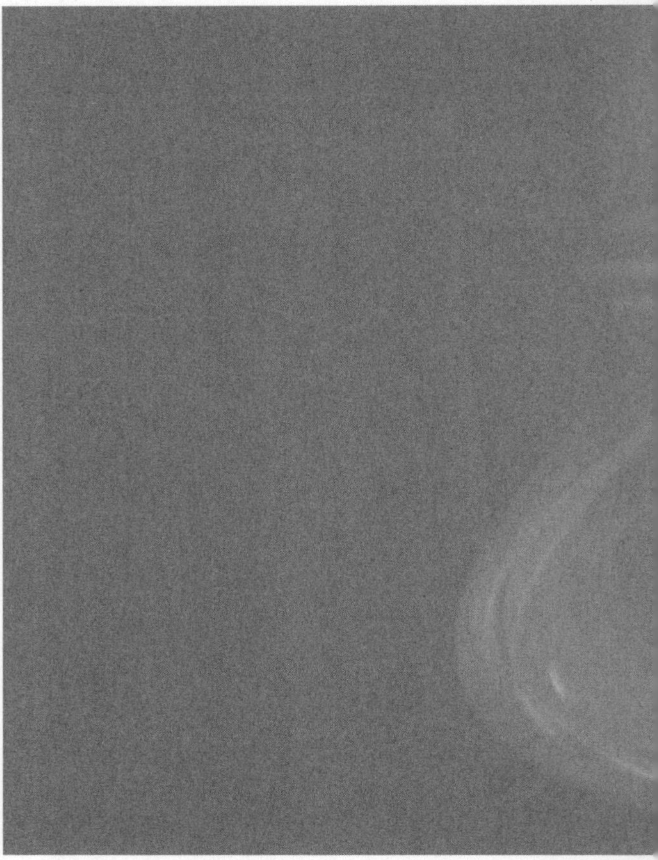

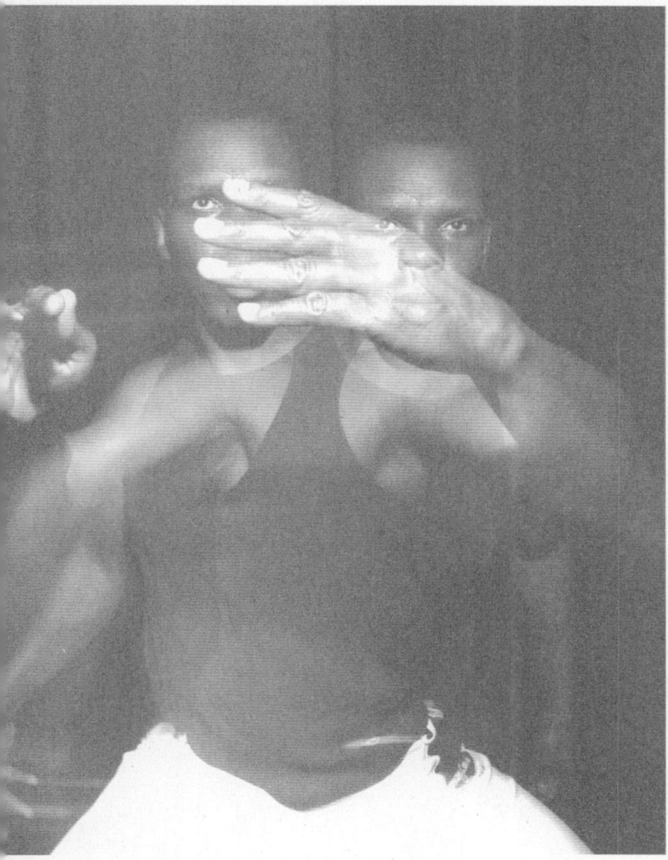

Olu Taiwo, photo: Dan Reid.

collective

artificial friendship

Lilia Mestre

⇛

Dear you,

How are you? Here is an excerpt of a letter I wrote during the first confinement, April 2020 when I was invited by Roselle Pineda / PCI to give a talk about curatorial approaches in time of halting and transformation. I would like to share this with you because I'm interested in what you think about it.

My practice as a curator consists of creating a correspondence between several artistic researchers through a combination of presentations and writing practice. We address each other not directly as in a normal feedback activity, but with the delay of the letter, the delay of reflecting on what a critical response could be and how we want to formulate it, with which language.

The delay of the letter produces criticality⊕→ as a modality of care. I'm holding on to you, while responding to your work. I carry you with me. I think through you. You change me. I'm totally in love with the idea that a critical world is a world of change. An inclusive environment of transformation.

I call for *artificial friendship*.

This concept is a paradox, a provocation, and an attempt to give attention to how to engage with concerns, people and materialities that are not ours and might not seem interesting at first view because they don't address us directly.

I call for artificial friendship, and here you are. I open up the potential of friendship with you to be able to make myself available to write to you. I've been thinking about the concept of artificial friendship after creating scores (see scoring↬) as an infrastructure for encounter in which I could observe and experiment with a relational shift in the approach to others. A mode of relation that is based on taking seriously, and accepting as a valuable companion in life, that what doesn't correspond directly to my understanding of the world. To take into consideration not the symbiotic but intra-dependent relationships, the close and the far at the same time. The known and the unknown and the in-between.

I call for artificial friendship as a form of dedication to the unknown. A form of care for the ones we don't know. Dear stranger, how are you? How do you feel? What do you do? ⇒

I've been asking myself; how can friendship and artificiality be partners towards an infrastructure of care for the other. Paradoxical at first instance, both these concepts, if allied, can create the conditions for a sociability of commitment, dedication, attention, patience, and inclusion. I have been working with scores9→, in their artificiality, to set a series of scheduled moments in time and space with clear constraints, where one can perform what friendship does, and even become art[ificial] friends, without there having to be a friendship in the first place.

This is an invitation to spend time together. To meet in a place that offers availability and the moment of being present to each other. The sort of agreement one can commit to when visiting a friend. I would like to propose that we think thoroughly about this when we think about curatorial and performing approaches. About spaces and conditions that introduce forms of attendance that are not consumeristic but involve the vulnerability of coming together, as a form of care for the other. A form of care for a complex societal ecosystem that can embrace change.

If you'd like to get back to me you can reach me at lilia@apass.be

Looking forwards to reading from you.
Warmly,
Lilia

babanton art

the good neighbours agree to always agree

Bunga Siagian & Ismal Muntaha
(Jatiwangi art Factory)

⇛

The word *saling bantu* (mutual assistance) is meant to separate it from the terminology 'collaboration', 'participation', 'involvement', 'cooperation', words that are widely used to explain community-based art practices. Not only do those words arise from a different context in the art scene, but in the context of language they are also not sufficient to explain the situation of Jatiwangi, as the rural centre of Indonesian clay production. *Saling bantu* is the Indonesian translation for the Sundanese *babanton*, which unfortunately does not capture its precise meaning, nor does the English translation 'helping each other' (translator's note: 'mutual assistance' or 'mutual aid' may be more appropriate terms, although they still may not capture the full extent of the meaning). *Babanton* is distinct from the words collaboration, joint work, *gotong royong* (the well-known ethos in Indonesia regarding collective work), and other similar words that presuppose as well as rely on goodwill, willingness, agreement, and the need to do something together. However, it has its limitations: it applies to collective needs (not personal needs, therefore it is often institutionalized by the state). It is spontaneous and current (of urgent needs, such as clearing clogged sewers, and so on), and cannot be romanticized as an ever-present value in a community.

Babanton is a game. It is crucial to understand the gameplay. First, from its terminology: in Sundanese, 'help' (*Indonesian: bantu*) is translated as 'banton', but the word *babanton* contains a repetition of 'banton'. It means the help is reciprocated, like in a game. *babanton* is a societal value in Jatiwangi. As a game, it starts from individual needs. In neighbourhood social practices, as a good neighbour, it is a social obligation to help a fellow neighbour who is having *hajat* (event, ceremony, errands). Therefore, we need to sacrifice our 'time', even if it's work time. It subsequently establishes a social 'currency' that uplifts our dignity as people living in a community. A help from our neighbour, as a currency, may be exchanged in times of need.

JaF artistic practices engage with the spirit of the community's *babanton*. In the early days of JaF, many initiations or art projects were nothing but but *hajatan* ⇛ presented by JaF that were held by Arief Yudi's family —a distinguished family in the village (his brother Ginggi was the Village Head at the time). The neighbours acted as good neighbours to do *babanton* in the artistic activities, whether they understood them or not, needed them or not. What they knew was that the neighbour was having a *hajat* and was in need of help. Afterwards, automatically, JaF would also be involved in this mutual assistance game by being a good neighbour, from providing a sound system and a stage on a neighbours' *hajat*, designing logos for neighbours' products, making or editing videos, documenting pre-wedding photos, to merely fixing printers. One time, Ginggi blurted, 'Any talk of art in society without ever helping a neighbour's *hajat* or attending a neighbour's funeral is utter baloney.'

Let's imagine that JaF's neighbours are also other community members, local governments (at least Arief Yudi's schoolmates or Ginggi), roof tile factory entrepreneurs, police, and other institutions⊕↣. Then, automatically, they will be involved in the *babanton* arts that manifest in the ever-expanding collective artistic practices, in which *tanah*↣ is exalted within. This interplay between art and *babanton* enriches them both; art expands the *babanton* practice into not just an individual matter—celebrating a marriage or making a house is being turned into larger collective works. On the other hand, *babanton* restores art to an important position in creating the imagination and action of a living space that is good for collective life.

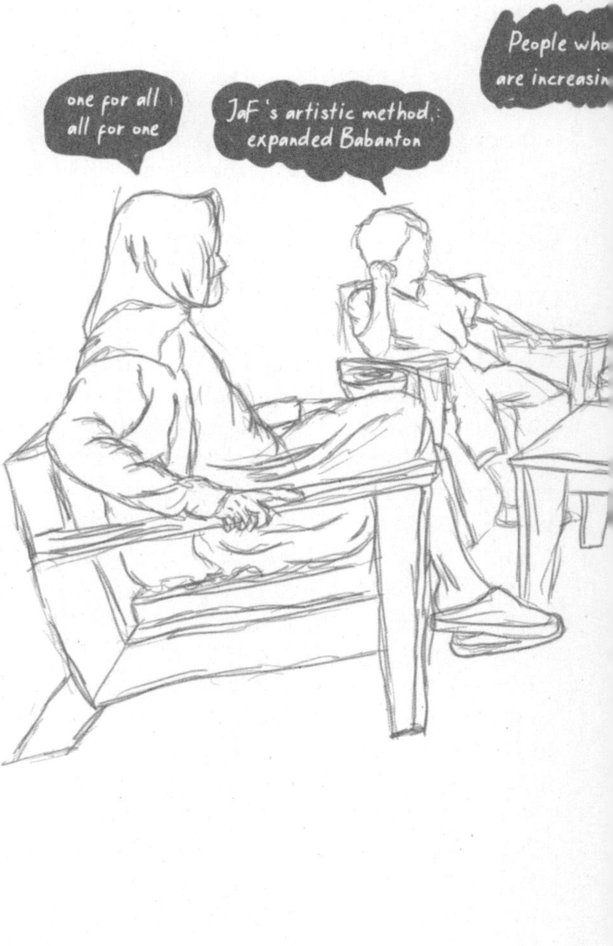
one for all
all for one
JaF's artistic method:
expanded Babanton
People who
are increasin

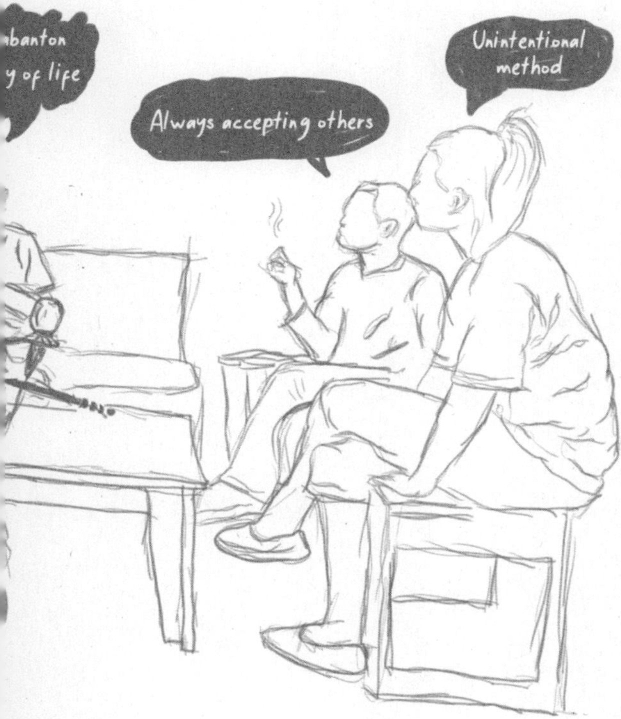
banton
y of life
Always accepting others
Unintentional
method

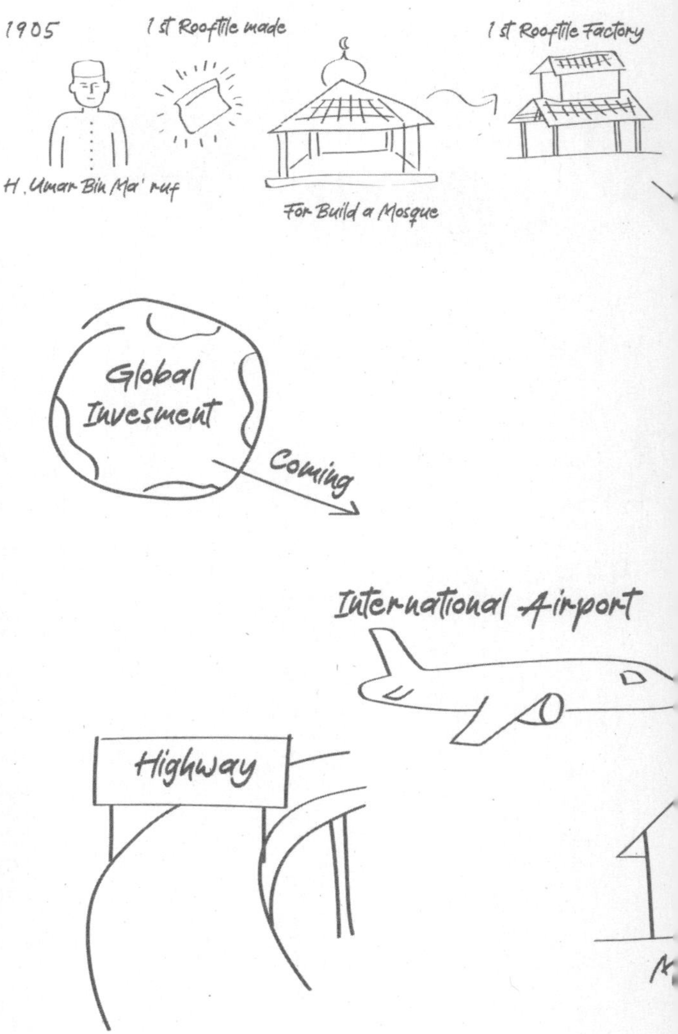
1905
1 st Rooftile made
1 st Rooftile Factory
H. Umar Bin Ma' ruf
For Build a Mosque
Global Invesment
Coming
International Airport
Highway

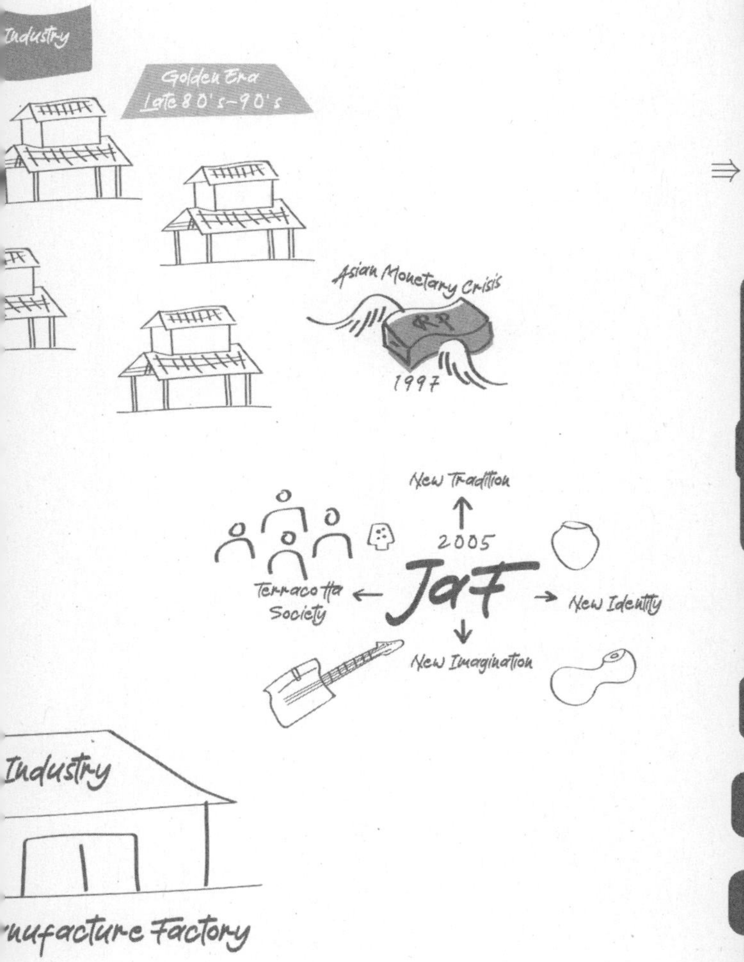
Industry
Golden Era
Late 80's–90's
Asian Monetary Crisis
1997
New Tradition
2005
JaF
Terracotta Society
New Identity
New Imagination
Industry
nufacture Factory

collective organization

logistics part II

Elaine W. Ho & Florian Cramer

⇛

The following edited correspondence ran in parallel to shipment HQL-364 from Rotterdam to Hong Kong through the network of LIGHT LOGISTICS, and was preceded by the correspondence in distribution↣

EWH: I think the need to play with formats of work, organization, and distribution↣ are now more urgent than ever before—not because crisis is upon us, but because the problems that were always there have been revealed more blatantly. Why art, design, and culture are still important is because they deal with methodologies—comings together and ways of seeing and playing that precede the politics that most everyday folk don't even realize addresses (or neglects, or unfairly treats) them. So education, and welfare, and government funding all need to go through a self-reflexive hall of mirrors, so to speak.

FC: I couldn't agree more. At the same time, I'm afraid of the empty gestures⇢ and buzzwords that will get ticked off (like, for example, 'care' as a now-ubiquitous noun in art project funding application prose) if this becomes more mainstream. In Europe, I also witness the constant failure of artists to truly commit to collective projects and not just use them as platforms⇛ for displaying/performing their individual portfolios.

EWH: Yes, it is not surprising at all that we've watched the hype on care build up over the last year, but as someone primarily confined to margins, the mainstreaming of discourses is also something to learn and navigate as part of our practices. The tricky thing about care, and so many other widely debated issues is that they really need to be enacted rather than simply theorized or talked about. But the need to repeat, repeat, and repeat again to people who are less affected by what is lacking in the socioeconomic system (power is a crux issue at every scale) is a necessary part of expanding possibility. It entails 'mainstreaming' and popularizing and this gives those of us who do want to speak and practice from a position without power a tremendous pressure to re-circuit, re-articulate, and re-work the existing imaginaries.

What you mentioned about the failure to really collectivize in Europe is also a problem in Hong Kong and China. When HomeShop, the artist-run project space I was involved with from 2008–2013, was invited to participate in the 'Unlived by What is Seen' exhibition in 2014, the curators told us they wanted to include us as a collective practice because they felt that all the other collectives they observed in China at the time were merely solidarity-for-opportunity kinds of conglomerations, often splitting up when the group becomes famous enough that the individuals of a group can then make their way with solo careers.

So it's no wonder that so many of us have that starry-eyed fascination with the hype of many Indonesian collectives, *haha*, but as discussed with my friend Riar Rizaldi in a talk a couple of weeks ago, there are many problems there as well that tend not to get discussed publicly, and the exportation of *nongkrong* can in some ways be just as much of a selling strategy like anything else.

That said, having much more time to read and dilly-dally around in a confined space these days, I finally got to read your paper on 1970s Mail Art more carefully, and the key value I can take from the various examples you present is to see similar struggles and resonances resulting in similar impulses and tactics, such that your idea of the 'eternal network' represents a notion of affinity.

FC: Yes, and I am also wondering whether these struggles, resonances, and mistakes need to be constantly re-enacted and repeated by each new

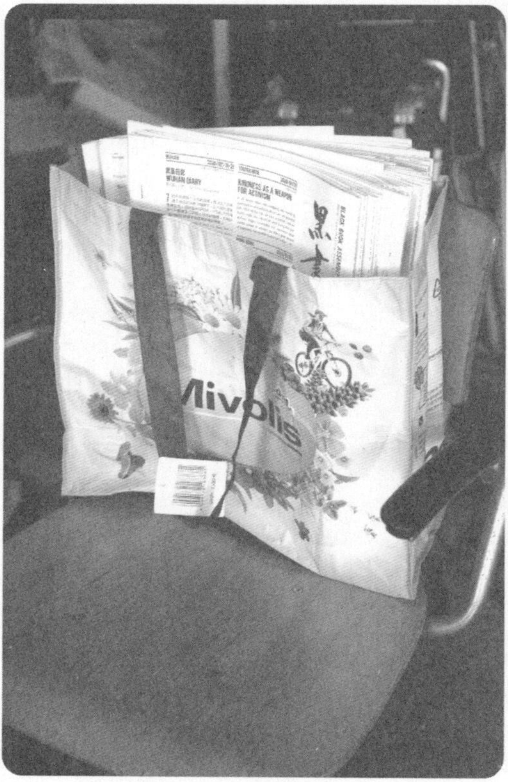

LIGHT LOGISTICS shipment HQL-364,
photo: Florian Cramer.

generation in order to be fully (*i.e.* not just in an abstract or disembodied manner) understood.

EWH: There are changes along the way, from generation-to-generation mutation. But I fear that despite such continuities, there is also a repetitive relegation to the realm of marginal play. Whatever foresight those projects from the sixties forward had for internet behaviours today—and as you say our pinpointing of AI/algorithms as the evils of the system is misplaced—how could intimate and networked actions parasitizing off of larger infrastructures really affect anything?

FC: Maybe that's the problem—that, by focusing on (larger societal) effects, we're unintentionally superimposing growth or impact expectations on these projects while their main value might have been their subjective-collective experience, and functioning as an experiment?

EWH: Thank you for the reminder. I have to tell myself again and again in so many arenas to focus upon 'subjective-collective experience, and functioning as an experiment', rather than the unintentional but hard-to-escape notions of growth, development, and impact, as you say. The question of change is perhaps naïve and misplaced. Regardless, it is difficult not to acknowledge outcomes as part of the process of communication that happens among any form of *collective organizing*. How that communication occurs is central to the difference between centralized or decentralized processes, and I think Display Distribute's inquiry into grey economies actually implicates us within certain murky areas between centralization and decentralization. These have been some of the greatest challenges to the project, but they are reasons to continue. You are right that 'radical inclusivity' does not necessarily garner any momentum, but neither do elitism and the reverse snobbery of oligarchic movements, which is a critique of both ends of the political spectrum.

If as you say the main value is located in the experiment of a subjective-collective experience, then your previous question might be answered by saying that the constant re-enactments and repetitions by new generations *are* necessary. Embodiment and affect cannot be historically reviewed except as practiced singularities, right?

FC: Yes, but you could also criticize that as a petty-bourgeois hobbyist self-limitation that gives up on the larger picture.

EWH: Completely on the mark as well! There is a close friend with whom I have had many emotional disputes along these lines, and perhaps this pinpointed critique precisely circles us back in some way—whether as a picture or a way of manoeuvring—to the necessities of an eternal network.

2021-02-19

Dear 慢遞員易拎何子 (& 妍廷),

HQL-364 is currently quarantined in a hotel in Taichung. Elaine, I hope it's not a major let-down that we have only been able to bag thirteen copies because of the bulkiness of Yenting's luggage. My agreement with courier Amy S. Wu was that she would give me a large stack of copies and that I would return to her whatever wouldn't fit the luggage. The remaining 62 copies are currently at my home and still need to be returned to Amy, who lives nearby.

Florian

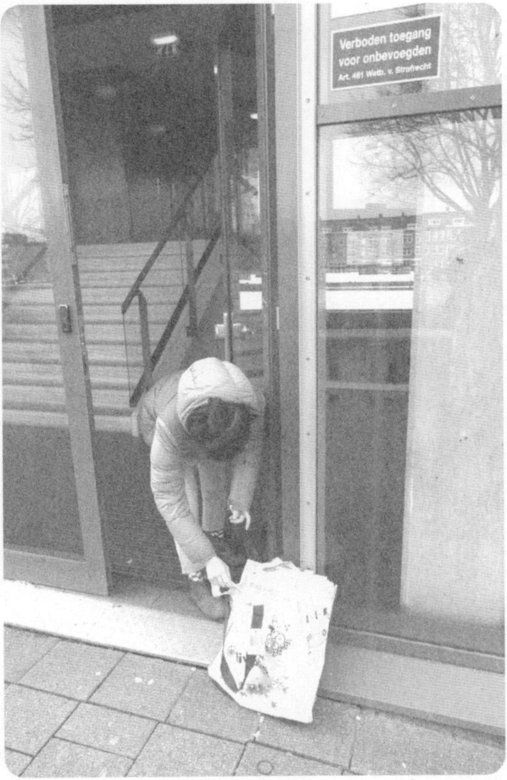

delivery of LIGHT LOGISTICS shipment HQL-364,
photo: Florian Cramer.

⇒

專頁 Headquarters　　出版物庫存 DISTRO　　後勤慢遞 LIGHT LOGISTICS

內容 CONTENTS //

黑書眾半年多帳
Black Book Assembly More-Than-Half-A-Year-in-Review

出發點 START POINT //

安卡拉
Ankara

定量信息 QUANTITATIVE DATA //

大概300份
approximately 300 copies

大概21.5公斤
approximately 21.5kg

慢遞人員 COU

官妍廷 KUAN Yen-Ting

Florian CRAMER

Merve BEDIR

Ruud & Jeannette
van MEETEREN

吳宗 Amy S. WU

Jock RHEA & Lara van

附注 NOTATION //

2021-02-22　下午 afternoon UTC+08：
慢遞員CRAMER先生的更新：「之前拿的大部分HQL-364的刊物今天還給Amy了；在
COURIER Mr. CRAMER's UPDATE: *Most of the zines from HQL-364 went back to Amy today.*

HK$ 0.00 0 items

號碼 DISPATCH № //

HQL-364

⇒

END POINT //

Kong

ung

stanbul

· Amsterdam

terdam

kok

物流情況 SHIPPING STATUS //

運送中 IN TRANSIT

慢遞招募發布
ROUTE REQUESTED :
2020-03-03，18:07

在附件，
ocumentation of the transfer (a distance of 1.6km)

cybernetic community

Baruch Gottlieb

⇛

The material practices↣ of many contemporary artist and activist collectives are strongly oriented towards, and embedded in, local communities. At the same time the concept of community has fundamentally changed through digital communication technology. It is a common assumption that non-digital local communities are distinct from digital global communities, but in fact the two are rather mutually and dynamically related in feedback loops of technical effects and social responses. This cybridity gives new urgency to the concept of community. Now, more than ever, it produces cultural and social tendencies and needs that defy expectations, place, and time.

Our actions have effects and these effects act back upon us in a learning process. While this is an uncontroversial statement, the age of hyper automation gives us the impression that this experience is massively compounded, as in a meta-butterfly effect, a feedforward hall of mirrors, or hell of mirrors. Our actions seem to have at once too little and too much consequence. How to get the right sense of scale in today's intensively networked environment? Community no longer seems to have continuity, but appears to be an ad hoc grouping which could just as well be otherwise. One can be a part of several 'communities' at once, and then just as suddenly, of several others. As a community, we act as intersections of multi-dimensional Venn diagrams where our world of associations reconfigures around us in real time.

Of course community still has a centre of gravity, its provisional situatedness. In tension with the networked context, every member of a community has its own situatedness, if only in that of their physical body or device. What happens if a social network is radically distributed, and no longer runs on a central server, as in the case of software projects like

Patchwork/SecureScuttlebutt? Then the network coheres around the chief maintainers of the project.

A community is always intractably material. What we would like to examine are the relationships and tensions between the participants and the material apparatus that entertains them. The physical space of the contemporary art institute West Den Haag ⇒ includes an 'Alphabetum' which could be called a proto-institutionality dedicated to the forms of letters (grammatography↣). The community around the Alphabetum coalesces around its physical space, just as a community of an online social network coalesces in its respective physical space, i.e., its servers.

The Alphabetum functions as a laboratory for *cybernetic community* knowledge creation, the generation of unlikely and unexpected forms of expression and exchange. Also, as it is cybernetic, it is committed to storage, archiving as a recursive practice in a kind of communal learning. The exhibitions in the Alphabetum are probes sent out into the community for responses, which are processed and built into subsequent exhibitions. Through this recursive feedback process, the Alphabetum 'learns' about the environment that is interested in the programme. At the same time, it is instrumented by the public to respond to their interests. This community exercise is concretized in the exhibits on display in the Alphabetum, which are subsequently curated and recontextualized by the community.

platform

Anja Groten

⇛

a *platform* design request

In recent years the Hackers & Designers collective[1] has been frequently approached by organizations and initiatives from the fields of art, design, technology, and academia with the question: 'Do you want to design our platform?' An intricate question as the term platform refers to a multitude of phenomena and objects. The platform's ambiguity seems particularly amplified when articulated as part of a design brief, suggesting that the platform is to be an expansion of the realm of designed *things*.

An organization as platform supports individuals or groups in addressing an audience. In a computational context, the term platform refers to a technical infrastructure, for instance an environment in which software applications are designed, deployed, or used, such as computer hardware, operating systems, gaming devices, mobile devices.[2]

With the H&D collective we have designed, built, and maintained technical infrastructures, such as software, webware, and services that enable online collaboration, production, organization, and publishing of digital content. Such diy⇝ platforms are tool convergences that—in their particular composition—cater to the particular needs of the collective. They are content

1. Hackers & Designers is a non-profit workshop⟼ initiative organizing activities at the intersection of technology, design, and art. The larger H&D community consists of a growing pool of international makers from diverse backgrounds. The aim of H&D is to stimulate and support exchange, learning and collaborations within this larger network of soft- and hardware developers, designers, artists, and researchers, and to create inspiring and encouraging spaces for the community to share skills, urgent topics, and interests, as well as concrete offers for commissions, exhibitions, guest lectures and workshop⟼ facilitation.
2. Tarleton Gillespie, 'The Politics of "Platforms"', *New Media & Society* 12, no. 3 (May 2010), pp. 347–64.

management systems,[3] chat applications,[4] collaborative writing tools,[5] online spreadsheets[6] and file sharing systems.[7] These self-made, appropriated or hacked tools and systems are implicated in the ways the members of the collective work together. H&D's technical infrastructure continuously evolves, and at times fails, or acts in an unexpected way. H&D shapes and reshapes its modes of organizing around the possibilities and limitations of such self-made platforms—along with learning to cope with system incompatibilities, broken links, expired protocols, and unreliable backups. Therefore, the notion of platform is at the core of its existence. ⇛

The platform-design request implies that a platform can be regarded as separate from its context, and that there is a causal relationship between platform and design. However, because of how the H&D collective has developed relationships with technical infrastructures it would be difficult to disconnect the technical aspects from the organizational and social aspects of platforms. The question then arises whether platforms—in the way we relate to them at H&D, as an inherent part of the collective's fabric, including its characteristic of constant emergence, spontaneity, and unreliability—can be designed at all?

In my view, the question: 'Do you want to design our platform?' wrongly implies a certain fixedness, a beginning and an end of a digital platform and the possibility to foresee a platform's trajectory. The 'commissioners' who formulated the request position themselves as end users of the platform, and

3. hackersanddesigners.nl/s/Publishing/p/The_making_of_hackersanddesigners.nl.
4. hackersanddesigners.nl/s/Tools/p/Chattypub.
5. hackersanddesigners.nl/s/Tools/p/Free_Wiki.
6. hackersanddesigners.nl/s/Tools/p/H%26D_Ethercalc.
7. hackersanddesigners.nl/s/Summer_Academy_2020/p/Becoming_a_Server.

suggest some kind of ownership of it. It would be 'their' platform that 'we' are designing. However, a platform, as I see it, in its manifold of meanings is interwoven in collective practice and cannot be owned.

thinking with platforms

Besides its technical connotations, the term platform is also often used figuratively, for instance referring to organizations such as H&D. As such, it tends to assign an assumed value to the platform-organization as supportive and enabling, and risks a flattening of the technical and organizational particularities and implications of a collective. The question is how to think *with* the various meanings of 'platform'? How do platform's different (technical, organizational, architectural, political) connotations intersect—act together and apart?

In 2020, H&D developed a physical structure,[8] the 'H&D platform', together with architectural designer Thomas Rustemeyer. The installation was meant to represent the H&D collective in its endeavour to bring together different practitioners, artists, designers, and computer programmers[9] and facilitate exchanges among them. The platform would be activated at different moments, for instance as a workshop↦ space, a stage for performances and presentations, and as a reading room.

8. Tetem – Presentatieruimte & platform voor Digitale cultuur en MaakCultuur, tetem.nl/.
9. Contributing artists: Nazanin Karimi, Kiki Mager, The Underground Division (Jara Rocha, Helen Pritchard, Femke Snelting), Thomas Rustemeyer.

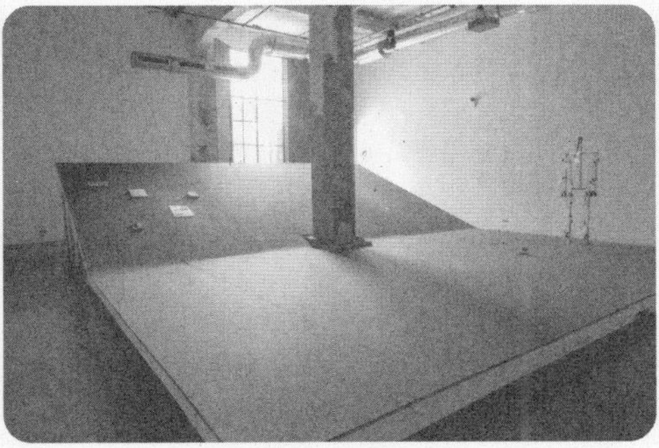

H&D platform installation, Tetem Enschede, May 2020.

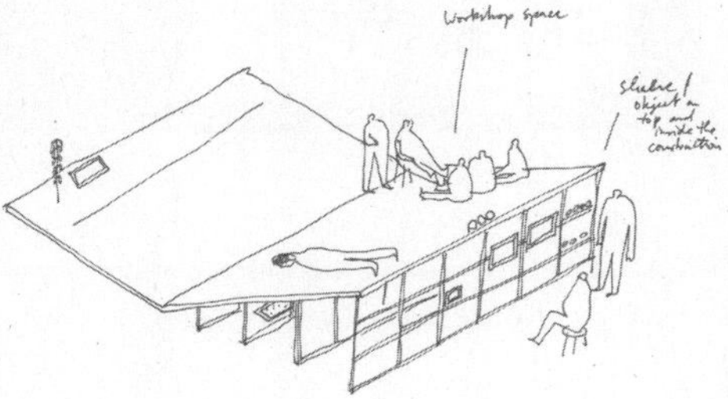

Sketch by Thomas Rustemeyer, 2020.

However, due to the global Covid-19 pandemic the platform as we had initially envisioned it remained more or less unvisited and untouched. Yet, through the sudden need for our planned activities to continue online, we developed other, digital, means of pursuing our activities. For instance, we created a project website that showcases the work of the contributing artists[10] and draws together their research and process documentation. We furthermore developed the 'H&D livestream platform' as we witnessed an increasing fatigue of commercial platforms. The fatigue is caused by large tech companies such as Google, Facebook, Microsoft or Zoom, who profit from their user's reliance upon them in times of crisis by selling their data.[11]

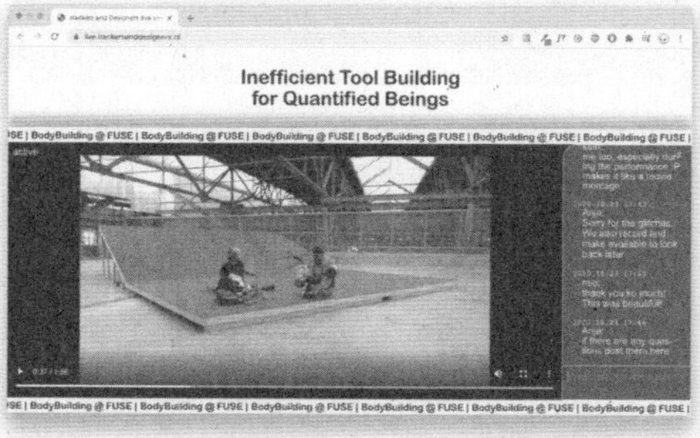

H&D livestream platform and the physical platform installation, NDSM FUSE, October, 2020.

The H&D livestream platform converges an open-source streaming software, a streaming service, and a chat interface.[12] Certainly less clumsy 'off-the-shelf' platforms do exist. The H&D livestream platform 'acted up' and caused moments of discomfort through its glitches and lags. However, it sustained its appearance,

10. bodybuilding.hackersanddesigners.nl/.
11. theverge.com/interface/2020/4/2/21202984/zoom-backlash-zoombombing-encryption-exploits-consumerization-of-it; www.cyberscoop.com/zoom-fbi-teleconference-hijacking/; www.techradar.com/reviews/zoom.
12. hackersanddesigners.nl/s/Tools/p/H%26D_livestream.

and has hosted many online H&D events in different contexts.

In the context of H&D, the collective seems to establish intrinsic relationships with digital tools and technical infrastructures that expand the realm of utility. An important part of building and maintaining such relationships are the manners in which the collective copes with unreliability, exercising patience and curiosity towards unintended technical glitches. In such a context, platforms can therefore not be described as self-contained entities. They travel between a multiplicity of meanings and inhabit collective peculiarities, as they are designed and redesigned in action and through interaction, which, in my view, makes it impossible to uphold a user-designer distinction. ⇛

To recap, a self-organized collective such as H&D shapes itself through technical infrastructures. In turn, technical infrastructures also continuously evolve with the collective, oftentimes in unpredictable ways. The emerging technical infrastructure around the aforementioned exhibition project is an example of that. Through their co-evolvement with collective practice, such platforms can therefore not be described as disconnected from collectivity.

public time

Eleni Kamma

⇛

Public time: a period of a shared experience of an action taking place in common view, relating to, or being in the service of the common interest, during which the viewer's agency is consciously enabled and mobilized through the physical relationship of his/her self to others. Public time is measured in the presence of witnesses, whereby humans and/or material things (recording devices and documents) serve as and certify evidence or proof. In an art practice, public time includes both the time needed for preparing an event or action and the event or action itself, which are made visible to and shared by an audience, either live and/or through media registration.

The term public time is relevant for the notion of parrhesia—meaning the courage to speak one's mind—and for parrhesiastic practices, which I approach as exercises, understood in the ancient Greek context of *askesis* or disciplined practice. These exercises aim at finding the courage to speak one's mind by positioning and expressing oneself in relation to others. This happens through an expanded version of performativity that focuses on the right of the people (non-privileged as much as privileged) to 'appear' and on the potential of technology and virtual participation to enable the appearance of these bodies. In the field of art, parrhesiastic practices often reveal uncomfortable truths about conventions by undoing dignity and seriousness. They aim at engaging and affecting the spectator through various strategies, ranging from playful, friendly, and healing, to confrontational, disruptive, or aggressive. Unlike trolling phenomena taking place in online social communities, for the one who practices parrhesia this revealing of uncomfortable truths needs to be coupled with some kind of implication, engagement, self-exposure, and a sense of personal responsibility and shame. At that very moment in which the parrhesiast speaks boldly, not only does he/she tackle truth and existing power relations, but also his/her own subjectivity. In finding the courage to examine one's self and by putting his/her beliefs to the test on a daily basis, the one who practices parrhesia is freed from previous experiences, prejudices, and forms of control imposed on him/her through the 'common opinion'. In this ⇛ sense the parrhesiast is constantly subjected to self-transformation and/or self-de/reconstruction.

In *Philosophy, Politics, Autonomy: Essays in Political Philosophy* (1991), Greek-French philosopher Cornelius Castoriadis defines public time in a historiographic sense and discusses parrhesia in relation to the 'project of autonomy.' Two roots exist within the Greek word autonomy: autos (εγώ ο ίδιος = myself) and nomos (law). An autonomous person creates his/her own law. Castoriadis argues that the first political society in which the citizens took the responsibility for their way of living and for legislatory regulations of social relations was in Ancient Greece. He posits that the possibility to ask questions as an individual or a group regarding social institutions-⊕→ occurred for the first time in Athens in the fifth century BCE. In this tradition, citizens contribute to the creation of public space (and public time) through the co-existence of three necessary and decisive phenomena: courage (*parrhesia*), responsibility (*euthini*), and shame (*aidos, aischune*).

In my presentation at the Making Matters Symposium (November 2020), I considered Etherpad as a tool for co-creating public time. Between February 16 and March 21, 2021, Thalia Hoffman (TH) and myself (EK) further discussed the term.

Public

Who is the public? 'Public' here is an adjective defining the type of time. But indeed, who is the public in the case of a public artistic event? Is this type of open participation enough to create a shared sense of collectivity among the participants? What does a shared sense of collectivity contain? I suggest each participant needs to see/feel their contribution to the collective, which can be at the same time seen/felt/inspected by the collective body⇢ of participants, enhancing in this way an understanding of individual contribution as responsibility.

Time

The Etherpad is an open-source online text editor. Each user's contributions are indicated by a colour code and are recorded onscreen in real time. Unlike discussions in a physical gathering (where unspoken communication expressed through facial expressions and bodily gestures⇢ accompanies words) or cloud-based platforms⇛ for video conferencing (where participants stare at each other's faces, talking heads videos arranged next to each other) communicating through the pad takes place purely on the level of ideas and the ability to relate mentally. Do only words communicate ideas? Words communicate ideas on the pad, but also something about the thinking process, the doubts and the hesitations involved in it: the movement of the interactions between our words, the time gaps, the mistakes, the erasures and re-writings. So maybe the pad (public space) needs to collect these gaps, doubts, and hesitations, and not erase them? It is not the pad that collects the gaps, doubts, and hesitations, but all participants together that make use of it to create this collection. But this is also what makes the pad a vulnerable tool for collecting content; any participant can erase the content with one click. Everyone can see what is written at the same time. The thought process is revealed, how thinking takes shape through typing. Does the typing change the thinking as well? Yes, the typing may change the thinking, provided one enters the pad in a state of mind open to change/dialogue, not set on a prefixed message one wishes to convey. I agree, being open for dialogue is needed many times for the possibility of change. I wondered though if the actual physical act of typing also changes the course of thinking. If we had a conversation with spoken words instead, would this change our thinking about concepts and ideas? I am not sure it would change our thinking about concepts, but there is this mechanical, repetitive aspect within the typing process that might interfere with one's course of thinking. It provokes people to react to each other on the spot. You type something and it is immediately there. Can this be described as performative writing? Yes! I feel we need to capture the 'liveness' of this performance. Something that reveals its becoming. Maybe recorded typing? Or performative co-typing that has the potential to be recorded? You can go back and erase it, but people can see this as everything is documented immediately. Online/digital media make it difficult to read each other, as the senses are limited to sight and hearing. Through this visualization of thought, it is feasible to collectively write and speak, to influence our thinking, to both witness and testify. I am interested in considering the pad as a tool for creating public time. Can it grasp collectivity in these times? Does collectivity need public time? or vice versa? Maybe they are interdependent? Collectivity needs public time to reflect on and inspect its own past actions, but also public time cannot exist without a collectivity. What do you think? I think there is an element of time that is always shared. What makes it public in the sense we are trying to capture here, is that the 'public' is doing something additional together during this time, something that is more than spending time together. Maybe we should ask what needs to happen in time to make it collective? I agree. Maybe it has to do with future decisions, actions, experiences that will have an effect on people, both individually and collectively.

Are we trying to create public space here? Since we are working on the same text but at separate times? I think what we are trying to do here is creating both public space *and* public time. This is how I became interested in Castoriadis, because he brings public time in the conversation as going hand-in-hand with the creation of public space. He finds these two indispensable for what he calls 'the project of autonomy'* of Ancient Greek democracy. I connect this with my suggestion to connect the personal to the shared, and through that define the collectiveness of this time.

Can time be private? Yes. When I am daydreaming, reading a book, or drawing, I withdraw to a personal sense of time, and I don't feel the need to share this with others. But this happens within a 'bigger' time that is public and local. The personal sense of time is always part of the time of the day at the particular place where it occurs, meaning it is public and local. I also feel time is always private as much as it is public, even if I share time with others, there is always the way I sense the time we spend together. If 'public' goes hand in hand with being exposed/accessible to everyone, are obscure and concealed activities also part of public time?

zoöp

Klaas Kuitenbrouwer

⇛

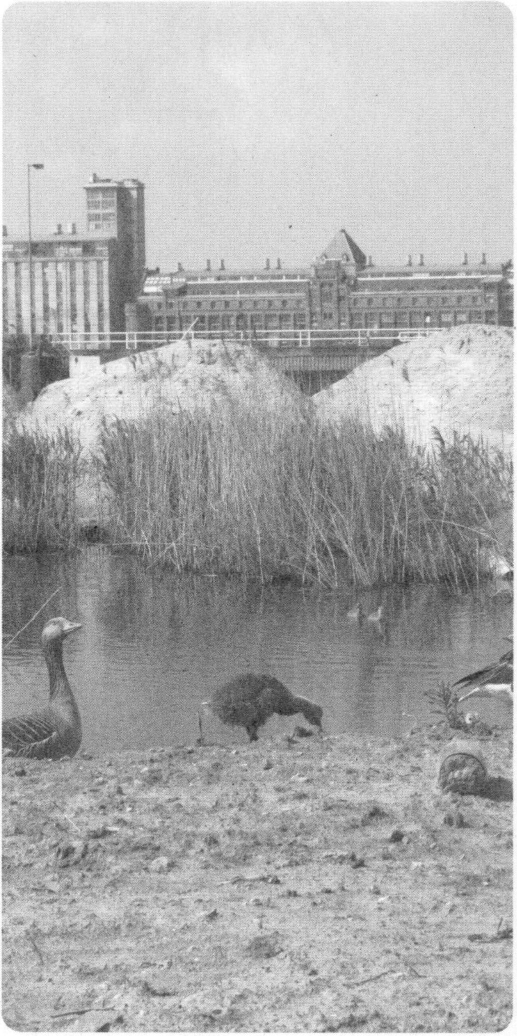

Photo: Patricia de Ruijter – mediakaal.nl.

The concept and practice of the *Zoöp* were developed between 2019 and 2021 by a network of artists, designers, philosophers, ecologists, and lawyers, initiated and led by Het Nieuwe Instituut in Rotterdam. Zoöp is short for zoöperation, a combination of the words cooperation and *zoë*, the Greek word for 'life'. Zoöp is a new organizational model or legal entity that allows organizations of many kinds to collaborate with other-than-human life in their own operational sphere. Zoöp is intended as an attempt to begin with the work of repair amidst the present-day climate catastrophe and escalating ecological degradation. It is a pragmatic answer to the issue of capitalist realism—i.e., the capitalist reductive understanding of the world as a collection of standardized commodities and scalable procedures. According to writer and cultural theorist Mark Fisher and philosopher Federico Campagna this understanding has become a metaphysics,[1] which led Fisher to the statement that '[i]t is easier to imagine the end of the world than the end of capitalism'.[2] ⇛

The sound of the desperate voices of collectives of animals, plants, and other bodies alive today can be harsh to the senses, and it demands an effort and dedication to take those voices into account.[3] The Zoöp way of working aims to concretize this effort. It has three goals: firstly, to strengthen the political and legal standing of other-than-human life within human capitalist societies. Secondly, to support ecological regeneration, in Zoöp vocabulary: Zoöps want to develop the zoönomy↦ (a regenerative economy that secures

1. Federico Campagna, *Technic & Magic: The Reconstruction of Reality* (London, etc.: Bloomsbury Academic, 2018).
2. Mark Fisher, *Capitalist Realism: Is There No Alternative?* (Hampshire: John Hunt Publishing, 2009).
3. Eva Meijer, *Dierentalen* (Leusden: ISVW Uitgevers, 2020).

the quality of life of multispecies collectivities) within and surrounding Zoöps. Thirdly, the aim of the initiators is to make the Zoöp model widely adoptable and put into practice by a variety of organizations, from farms to municipalities, from hotels to cemeteries, from commercial enterprises to non-profit organizations. The Zoöp model is the centrepiece of the Zoöp movement and shapes anchoring bodies for the larger practice of zoönomy↦.

In order to facilitate the development of the Zoöp movement, two legal bodies have been founded in 2022. One is the Zoönomic Institute. Its task is to help organizations to transform themselves into Zoöps. It grants organizations the right to call themselves Zoöps. The other one is the Zoönomic Foundation. As laid down in its statutes, the Zoönomic Foundation has one task only: to articulate and represent the needs and interests of other-than-human life in the spatial and operational domain of Zoöps and to translate these into organizational decision making.

Organizations that turn into a Zoöp keep their existing function—a school remains a school, a farm remains a farm, a hotel a hotel—but set themselves an additional goal, which is to foster zoönomy↦. An organization can be be accredited as Zoöp[4] by doing two things: first it grants the Zoönomic Foundation an observer seat on its board (or whatever body in charge of its policies). This seat is then filled by a human Speaker for the Living. The Speaker for the Living is bound to the statutes of the Zoönomic Foundation and acts as the speculative and political organ for other-than-human life in the Zoöp. Secondly, the organization commits itself to follow the Zoönomic annual cycle, by which it gradually transforms its operation, intervention

4. So, by the Zoönomic Institute, the central hub of the zoöp movement.

by intervention, into a regenerative practice that collaborates with other-than-human life and gives it space and opportunity to find quality of life.

The development of the Zoöp concept was inspired by the now famous Rights of Nature cases of Whanganui river, Mount Taranaki, and Te Urewera forest. These three collective other-than-human ⇒ bodies are the living ancestors of different New Zealand Iwi, tribes of the Maori, New Zealand's indigenous people. The river, mountain, and forest were granted legal personhood in the New Zealand jurisdiction between 2014 and 2017. In legal terms, they became incorporated other-than-humans. Whenever necessary, they are represented by human members of their respective Iwi.

In Western cultural tradition, collective bodies⇢ of other-than-humans do not have the status of ancestors. In fact, they are not even considered subjects, but resources, which caused the ecological disaster we find ourselves in. Although there is a growing movement of Rights of Nature legal and other activists, the legislative reform by which living other-than-humans should gain rights will be slow and thorny.

The Zoöp organizational format does not require the legislative reform that rights of nature require, but uses existing instruments of private law. Zoöp does not grant rights or personhood to living other-than-human entities but operates on the premise of them already having rights. Zoöp is intended as a way of organizing, a practice, a procedure that actively acknowledges these rights and the subjective experience of other-than-human life. It is focused on collaboration between human and other-than-human life. In this sense, the Zoöp model is a pragmatic shortcut to a Rights of Nature practice as it is established in the jurisdictions of Bolivia, Colombia, Ecuador, Uganda, India and many more countries, besides New Zealand.[5]

With the governance structure and the Zoönomic Foundation in place, a Zoöp, commits itself to figuring out how its operation can transform itself into a regenerative practice, contributing to the quality of life of a human inclusive ecology. It does so by following the Zoönomic annual cycle of four movements, called Demarcating, Observing & Sensing, Characterizing and Intervening.[6]

Demarcating answers the question: which (legal, human, organizational, and other-than-human) bodies form the Zoöp?[7] Demarcating situates the Zoöp's practice in its environment and articulates its locally specific questions for actual 'collective bodies→'.

Observing & Sensing is concerned with understanding the life-worlds of the different bodies that make up a Zoöp, and with the question of whether and how those bodies perceive and acknowledge each other's Zoöp participation.

Characterizing involves asking the question how the different bodies enhance or obstruct each other's quality of life. This will result in a first kind-of-diagnosis of the Zoöp's ecological integrity and exploration of interventions.

Intervening, then, is the process of actually changing the spatial arrangements, organizational practice or relational fabric of a Zoöp. Its primary objective is a local, thriving, combined human and

5. See for instance www.therightsofnature.org/what-is-rights-of-nature/.
6. zoop.hetnieuweinstituut.nl/instruments-methods.
7. Adopted and expanded from Elinor Ostrom's principles for managing commons onthecommons.org/magazine/elinor-ostroms-8-principles-managing-commmons, www.onthecommons.org/magazine/elinor-ostroms-8-principles-managing-commons.

other-than-human community that provides groundwork for other, more global aspects of the transformation of economy into zoönomy↦.

At the time of writing, more than twenty organizations (farms, cultural institutions⊕, holiday parks, educational institutions⊕ and others) have committed themselves to becoming a Zoöp. On 22 April 2022, Earth Day, Het Nieuwe Instituut in Rotterdam has become the first actual Zoöp in the world. ⇛

critique

criticality

Frans-Willem Korsten

Criticality⊕→ has been defined first and foremost within Marxist and post-structuralist frames, as an attitude and a praxis that aims to scrutinize and dismantle the dichotomies and hierarchies set up by ruling powers. Whereas these frames were philosophically inclined, other forms of criticality⊕→ were more practical. Often as a mix of both, distinct approaches were developed under the heading of, for instance, 'critical pedagogy', 'critical geography', or critical making↬. The following case offers different modalities of the term. The case concerns a public primary school, located close to a train station in Utrecht, a major city in the Netherlands. This had been the school's location since 1883. Children from lower and middle social classes had attended it, from a distinctly multicultural populace in the last decades of the twentieth century. Then, in the late 1990s, it had to make way for an office building, the so-called Klundertoren, named after the architect who designed it. The artwork on top of it from 2003, by Jan van Munster, reads IK—Dutch for 'I'.

The school was demolished and was offered a 'new' space in an old and decrepit building, classified as a 'monument' or listed building, opposite the original location. The renovation would partly be paid for by the real estate developer of the Klundertoren. After a disastrous process of moving the school into a building of which the renovation was not finished, the responsible councillor decided two years later that the school would have to move again, to make way for another X-tower. At this point, a group of parents said 'no'. Without knowing it at the time, they opposed a development project that involved an estimated investment of around 50 million euros. In a sense, they were critically unaware.

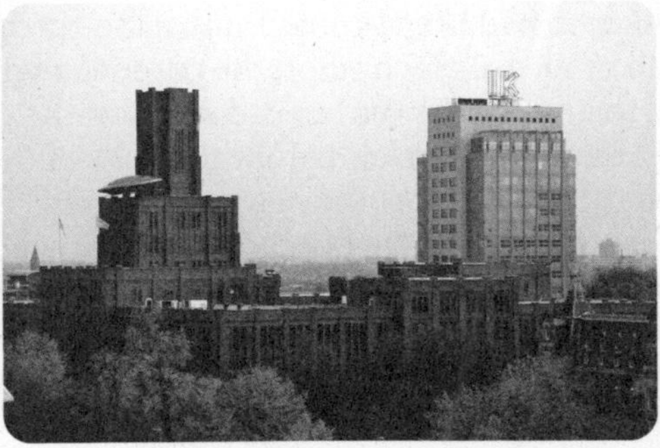

Klundertoren, Utrecht, photo: H. Boland, Utrecht Archive.

1. experiencing criticality ⊕›

Battles like these take a lot of time. One question is how long people are prepared to keep on fighting and stick together. For a real estate developer, five years, or ten years, or even fifteen years is nothing. On the contrary, years may add to profit. Let's call this the critical limit of perseverance. In this case, the battle would take five years.

Real estate developers may, on the face of it, function within the limits of the law, but are often closely allied with parties that do not. First, there were two clumsy, nightly attempts to set the listed building containing the school on fire. Then, during a gymnastics class of six- and seven-year-olds in the gym on the first floor, the stairway leading up to the gym was set on fire, as well as the doors to the emergency exit. An astute teacher grabbed a bench, pushed it through the window and helped the children escape via the roof of the neighbouring building. Let us call this the criticality ⊕› of the situation.

In a civil society, this is serious business. Now that their children had been brought into a life-threatening situation by an unknown actor, the parents might have decided to give up. Yet the burned shoes of the children that had been left before the door of the gym inspired them to contact the mayor, who in the Dutch system is in charge of the police. When the responsible councillor told the city council what had happened, there was a strange, chilling silence that had its political effect. The school was granted the permission to stay, and the building would be properly renovated. A fourth attempt to set it on fire did not have the desired effect either. As the council had taken its official decision, the critical moment had passed.

2. practicing criticality-⊕›

In the case at hand, criticality-⊕› consisted in the determination to take everything that the councillor or officials were saying as a subject of research, and to follow the money. It took the collective of parents two years of in-depth research, involving all the legal possibilities to acquire the necessary information, to find out that this specific school had to be removed because it was part of a substantial number of public-school buildings that were going to be sold and converted into apartment buildings. The funds thus obtained provided the municipality with the money needed for concentrating the city's entire vocational education in three new buildings. The latter may be a worthy cause. The question was why the money had to be found at the cost of public schooling, and at the cost of political and ethical transparency. The school buildings to be sold were often located in urban environments that over the past years had become impressively expensive, due to gentrification and economic developments. The municipality had to negotiate all sorts of agreements with real estate developers, who do not tend to spend public money cautiously and often operate in the shadows rather than in the full light of public scrutiny.

In response, the collective of parents decided to operate in the open. Every step they took was documented on a website: every plan, every letter, all arguments. When at some point the councillor tried to contact a member of the collective (me), and this parent engaged in a personal mail conversation, the parent was corrected by a good friend, also part of the collective, who was able to follow the conversation. And rightly so. It was a mail conversation that, because of its personal character, could easily lead to unofficial ⊕›
agreements, on the side, in the shadows, threatening the very transparency that was at stake. criticality⊕› involved the scrutiny of what others were saying and doing, and the attempt to be as open as possible to the critical assessment by others.

3. an ethics of criticality⊕›

Though the collective as a whole did not use the term explicitly, criticality⊕› proved to be a matter of defining it through praxis. During the height of the struggles, the collective would meet every two weeks, and discuss what to do, how to do it, and what not to do. Few parents involved had read Derrida, but in a sense,all were involved in a process of deconstruction since deconstruction is not something enforced *upon* something, but is always already at work in something, whether a text or situation. The *doxa* of real estate development and city council was already deconstructing itself through discursive cracks or contradictions that were made visible in the critical documentation process of the parents. It is helpful to re-read Derrida about the concept of deconstruction, here:

> ... deconstruction is neither an analysis nor a critique and its translation would have to take that into consideration. It is not an analysis in particular because the dismantling of a structure is not a regression toward a simple element, toward an indissoluble origin. ... No more is it a critique, in a general sense or in Kantian sense. The instance of *krinein* or of *krisis* (decision, choice, judgment, discernment) is itself, as is all the apparatus of transcendental critique, one of the essential ‹themes› or ‹objects› of deconstruction.[1]

The quote helps us first of all to distinguish between critique and criticality ⊕→. The first connotes the ability to decide, choose, judge, discern. The second connotes the fact that decisions, choices, judgments, and discernments are precisely the object or theme of deconstruction. The core of the struggle for the school was not to prove the municipality or its real estate allies wrong, but to show how the process of decision-making had been full of uncritical decisions, choices, judgments, and discernments. Secondly, it is worthwhile noting that the quote comes from a letter addressed to Toshihiko Izutsu, an expert on Zen Buddhism and Sufism, with a great interest in Truth (*Satori*, or Enlightenment). This truth, according to Izutsu, cannot be grasped by reason or language, nor

1. Jacques Derrida, 'Letter to a Japanese Friend', in *Derrida and Difference*, ed. David Wood and Robert Bernasconi (Warwick: Parousia Press, 1985), pp. 2–3.

can it be taught or understood intellectually.[2] It can only be a matter of praxis and process. Truth can never be discovered, then, although it can be momentarily experienced.

The fight for the school was not a spiritual matter. Or was it, at least in part? If criticality⊕→ was involved, it consisted in the desire to work towards truth—a truth that had two modalities. One the one hand it concerned a process of criticality⊕→ during which, in a certain sense, truth was found: the financial reality of agreements between the municipality, big educational institutions⊕→ and real estate developers. This truth does matter, as it may (but need not) increase the force of arguments. Yet it remains superficial without the ⊕→ veracity of a process, where truth is not to be discovered but to be experienced. Let's call this the ethics of criticality⊕→.

4. the situatedness of criticality⊕→

The specific case stands for a more general state of affairs. On all levels of government, the Dutch state has retreated from public tasks in the context of neo-liberal deregulation, propelled by the idea that 'the market' (a fiction) will do things better (a lie).

Critical making↬, in this context, with its focus on diy⇝ modes of making, holds a promise and a potential to serve the needs and desires of a multiplicity of people. In a sense, the entire struggle for the school was a matter of a political diy⇝. If the city council, if the councillor, if all sorts of public officials lack the agency or determination to adequately take care of public matters and public money, this provokes a diy⇝ response.

2. Kojiro Nakamura, 'The Significance of Toshihiko Izutsu's Legacy for Comparative Religion', *Intellectual Discourse* 17, no. 2 (2009), pp. 147–58.

Situatedness is of critical importance. The current form of capitalism is interested in anything that can make the system even more flexible, resulting in less stability for citizens, fewer rights, less care for labourers of all sorts. What is called deregulation often comes down to fuzzy forms of responsibility that make it difficult to follow money flows. The history of the Italian *precario bello* has been considered as a case in point. When in the seventies 'playing' and 'not sticking to the rules' became an important tool to deregulate state power, the economic response was that, *hey!*, playing and not sticking to the rules can be used to reconfigure labourers or employees, demanding them to become ever more creative in ever more precarious circumstances. Consequently, if diy was an instrument of the empowerment of people in the first instance, it also is a form that, in certain situations, can be cheaply appropriated or used as an excuse for more deregulation.

Criticality-⊕→, in this context, means the full awareness of a situation, an awareness of what is at stake, an awareness of the alternatives one is looking for in a forcefield dominated by others. It concerns the perseverance to critically assess what powers in charge are doing, and requires a practice of transparency that leaves one open to the criticality-⊕→ of others.

criticality

a conversation

Lilia Mestre & Pia Louwerens

Pia Louwerens: The notion of *criticality-⊕→* has accompanied me throughout my research with the workgroup material practices↣, not in the least because of the workgroup's initial interest in critical making↬. When my practice was embedded in West Den Haag[1] (see embeddedness⇢), one of my main questions became how to practice criticality-⊕→ from a position of proximity. When thinking about criticality-⊕→, my frame of reference is shaped by a.pass. a.pass is an educational platform⇛ for artistic research↬ based in Brussels (Belgium), where I participated in the post-graduate programme, and where I am currently involved as an Associate Researcher. Lilia Mestre is the artistic coordinator at a.pass. In the following, we will engage in a conversation to tease out what it actually is for us, this criticality-⊕→. In preparation for our talk, we read an interview with Karen Barad,[2] which we will refer to throughout our conversation.

Lilia, can you maybe start by saying how you think criticality-⊕→ is practiced at a.pass?

Lilia Mestre: We practice it in many ways. I don't think we are very interested in critique as an end in itself, so it's not about finding some weak spots that are most suitable for deconstruction. That would be a somewhat reductionist concept of criticality-⊕→. I do think that how we approach criticality-⊕→ entails deconstruction, but as a means of understanding the complexity that propositions bring to the fore. What kind of clusters, lines and apparatuses surround

1. West Den Haag, exhibition space in The Hague, www.westdenhaag.nl.
2. Rick Dolphijn and Iris van der Tuin, 'Matter Feels, Converses, Suffers, Desires, Yearns and Remembers. Interview with Karen Barad', *New Materialism: Interviews & Cartographies* (Ann Arbor, MI: 2 Open Humanities Press, 2012), pp. 48–70, dx.doi.org/10.3998/ohp.11515701.0001.001.

practices, performances, texts, and research and how and what do they produce as meaning?

I like the idea of consciousness as put forward by Karen Barad, as a conscious critical view; something that creates awareness could be called critical, right? Criticality⊕→ can be seen as a skill or a tool that develops a set of antennas—maybe antennas is a good metaphor. Seen this way, criticality⊕→ becomes a sensitive tool, responsive to what is proposed. I see criticality⊕→ as the desire to understand how to be involved.

PL: When I look up the etymology of 'critic' or 'critique', it leads to the Greek word krinein 'to separate, decide' which comes from a root that translates as 'to sieve', thus 'discriminate, distinguish'.[3] So, it's an interaction with an apparatus that makes a selection, or distinguishes. Funny actually, the two-slit experiment that Karen Barad bases her theory on is a sieving experiment as well, literally. It's the sieving that causes a diffraction pattern. According to Barad, studying the experiment doesn't tell you anything about the thing that you sieve, but you will know something about the phenomenon, which is the sieving plus the thing that came out. ⊕→

LM: Perhaps the understanding of the apparatus, whether a two-slit sieve or an artwork, makes visible what the performativity of the apparatus itself is. It's like a mise-en-scene of the apparatus. As in the apparatus of theatre, which contains the setting, the scenario, the operation itself including the audience.

PL: There's this really beautiful part in Barad's book,[4] where she wonders where the apparatus ends, and describes how there are no edges to it. Even the person seeing that mise-en-scene is part of the

3. etymonline.com/word/critic, accessed 5 April 2021.
4. Karen Barad, *Meeting the Universe Halfway* (Durham and London: Duke University Press, 2007), p. 143.

apparatus, the building that we're in is part of the apparatus, the printer that prints out the result is part of the apparatus, the people that funded the whole thing are part of it, the people sweeping the hallway. When you see things this way, there's this constant expansion.

For me criticality-⊕› holds this tension exactly, of a noting of difference and selection on the one hand, and constant expansion through awareness on the other. The selection or cut that it makes causes things to appear, and excludes other things.

Can you give an example how this resonates in a.pass?

LM: In a.pass, the participants are invited to be part of the institutional apparatus, somehow. They are part of the development of the practices generated in the institution-⊕›. We practice it in the sense that a.pass is not a stable structure. We have many institutional questions that arise from the participants' practices. We can take this one: 'what is criticality-⊕›?' and your invitation to write together. If we dig into this: How is this going to change our relations? Not just the existing relationship between the two of us but also the relation between the institutions-⊕› that are part of this publication, like West, the Workgroup and all the others participating. I think that a.pass as an institution-⊕› is shaped through the research practices that are present each moment, but also through how people deal with them and what their desire for criticality-⊕› is, how much they want to move through it or not. The capacity of listening. The desire to be confronted or not. I think all these things are determining what happens in a.pass and how content and infrastructures of research are interwoven.

PL: This idea that one can participate as a mode of criticality-⊕›, the idea of becoming part of the apparatus, is something that I clearly recognize as a practice in a.pass. In art education on often finds practices of critique for which the intentions of the artist have to be determined, to compare them to the work that either deviates from or falls in line with that intention. I was thinking that what seems different to me in the forms of feedback and critique that I experienced in a.pass, is the invitation to participate. I think Vladimir[5] once explained it to me as treating the group, or thinking of the group as a sort of extension of your body as a researcher, in that you are really invited into the apparatus. In turn you always consider how you invite others into your work, making them part of it. It takes away the illusion of the object of critique as separate from yourself as a participatory subject.

LM: The sense of participation in the context of criticality⊕› is also very important if we think about the audience that we want to address. Let's say that art is like the spectacle of phenomena, right; art exposes a certain phenomenon in certain conditions and invites people to attend through the conditions provided. I want the invitation, for me as an audience member, to be similar to the one that you described. I want to be able to participate, which doesn't necessarily mean active participation. But I want to know what is the invitation for me to respond and let feelings, emotions, thoughts, whatever it wants to create with me, appear. This is the potential of modifying it already, or at least to be able to be responsive to it.

How do you do that in your practice?

PL: As you know I'm very present in my work and my practice, as a subject that is an object as well. So, I read everything both through myself and with a kind

5. Vladimir Miller is an artist, researcher, scenographer and dramaturge. His practice aims at re-negotiating modes of spatial production within collaborative structures. He is a curator for the a.pass Research Center.

of distance. I see myself as practicing institutional critique, but it is inherently a critique of myself as part of the institution-⊕› or situation. This way I hope to invite others to consider their institutional entanglements as well.

LM: This is hard and very interesting work, because ultimately, you see yourself as an apparatus already, right, with a structure that conditions your power position, paradoxes, problems, and alliances. I think it's important to acknowledge that objects of study are complex objects and include the self and its context and background, including social class, gender, race, economic support, species, and so on.

The question is then: How can we create a soft distance which is set artificially, so it's a real artificial one (because what the hell is real?) that enables criticality-⊕›? This refers back to the baboon anecdote in the interview with Barad. A researcher of baboons decided to pretend to be a baboon—pretending became a tool to get in touch with her object of research, and actually be more objective.

I like to think of it as friendship (see artificial friendship⇛). Friendship opens to the possibility of diffraction, as Barad calls it. Then criticality-⊕› is not just about choosing or making distinctions, but it enables an accumulative process of relations that are critical in themselves. In the sense that one can think of criticality-⊕› itself as being a friend. Curious friends give you tools, open and close doors for elements that are already part of it, right, that you are already entangled with but have not seen yet.

PL: I'm starting to realize now that this is a mode of making, for me. Practicing criticality-⊕› creates so much material, all the time, and for me it is exciting to simply re-stage it in the place where I found it. It's like Barad's description of the expanded apparatus. To be with something and seeing, activating all your antennas, while taking into account how you are part of it, creates a kind of generative feedback loop, an abundance, in every singular situation. This is both a mode of criticality-⊕→ and source of creativity, if I may be so romantic to use that word. Now we're back to a.pass, because I think it's something that I got from you since you use this expression a lot, but it also really does 'open up'—a continuous folding and unfolding.

institution as practice

Pia Louwerens

institution as performative practice.
institution as an institutional body that performs and my body as an artist performing as part of it.
institution as something that I am entangled with and try to think about.
institution as whatever is instituted, or has instituted itself: a behaviour, a field, an agreement, an organization, plus the practice of instituting.
institution as midsize institutions such as art academies and exhibition spaces.
The nation state as institution.
Sitting as institution.
institution as enforced by the teacher who tells you to sit up straight.
institution as hard work.
institution as the place I met my ex.
institution as a combination of repetition and power.
institution as needing to be repeated, or reproduced repeatedly, in order to become instituted.
institution as needing power, authority, resources, attention—often from other institutions—in order to become instituted.
institution as instituting practice
institution as just starting out, but the origin is hard to pinpoint, since it emerges within a layered landscape of other institutions.
institution as a process of being instituted while instituting.
institution as a new groove being formed in a soup of existing infrastructures, because of a love affair between repetition and power.
institution as self-organization, which starts out as a new habit—not only do we meet once a week as a group, but we start imagining a future for ourselves as a collective. We think of a name, we start a Facebook page. We re-occur. We become legible as an institution, or as part of another institution. Perhaps we'll get

funding—resources and endorsement by institutions. We'll hire a space.
institution as having a dreamy, misty core, a collective imagination.
institution as something that never stops and is, truly, really, a practice.
institution as lines that need to be redrawn constantly before they fade, and are at risk of being drawn straighter by repetition.
institution as instituting—rewriting the text for our application.
institution as instituting—getting new uniforms.
institution as instituting—hiring a designer for our website.
institution as reproductive practice.
institution as needing, devouring, care, and attention.
institution as being held by many different people, objects, resources, infrastructures, practices, in many different ways and for many different reasons.
institution as the place where I go to give people guided tours.
institution as the place where I wear a hoodie with a text on it.
institution as saying 'we' when you are talking about it with friends although you only started working there one week ago.
institution as an orientational device—a path, starting out as informal but becoming more trodden. The more it is used, the clearer it becomes, and the easier it becomes to walk it.
institution as fortified habitus.
institution as infrastructure.
institution as both a result of (re)production, and a cause of it.
institution as self-preserving.
institution as precarious.
institution as self-referential.

institution as slow to respond to crisis or complaint.
institution as cutting machines that are as much defined by what they are as by what they aren't.
institution as both the path and the fence next to it and the impossibility to walk the bushy patch of field next to that.
institution as an apparatus that makes the cut for us, that makes us forget we do it time and time again.
institution as enacting a politics.
institution as conditional.
institution as empowering.
institution as identity.
institution as a character.
institution as a desire for comrades and just one moment of ease in this difficult life.
institution as giving us money.
institution as a condition enabling the simultaneity of performing the institution and resisting the very process of institutionalization.
institution as entangled with everything their practices produce, as phenomena.
institution as tending to forget themselves as they focus on what they produce.
institution as inside of us.
institution as a possessive spirit.
institution as architecture.
institution as impossible to leave.
(see embeddedness→)

representation

Feral Atlas (Lili Carr & Feifei Zhou)

Feral Atlas sometimes uses the term 'stories' to refer to how we tell things and so form knowledge. Our use of the term is to open up a discussion of genre. What kind of storytelling is most appropriate for the Anthropocene?

Feral Atlas is designed as an exploratory and open journey through an assembled polyphony of materials. Hand-painted watercolours, hydrophone recordings, molecular diagrams, scientific charts, sketches, sound art, and maps made from satellite data and calculated projections sit alongside scientific writing, autoethnography, memoir, poetry, biological modelling, music, video poems, and song. Each element provides an account of the Anthropocene in its own right. Yet when they come together, these diverse elements perform an iterative, multisensuous, and multiperspectival account of how imperial and industrial infrastructures make Anthropocene worlds.

Feral Atlas tries to forge an aesthetic that asks readers to linger over the gathered materials; to tell stories so beautifully that people stop to pay attention to what is going on, and to hold their attention to the scenes of action in which feral⇝ ecologies play out. Presenting materials with such absorbing detail, passion, and care that readers might become curious to know more, and in doing so become attuned, able to navigate and orientate themselves within a multidisciplinary array of representational modes.

During the symposium Making Matters: Collective Material Practices in Critical Times, we (Feral Atlas members Feifei Zhou and Lili Carr) conducted a workshop↦ in noticing feral⇝ effects in the area where you live. A screenshot of our collective online map of collated observations is reproduced overleaf.

Feral Atlas is curated and edited by Anna L. Tsing, Jennifer Deger, Alder Keleman Saxena and Feifei Zhou. It can be accessed online at Stanford University Press: www.feralatlas.org.

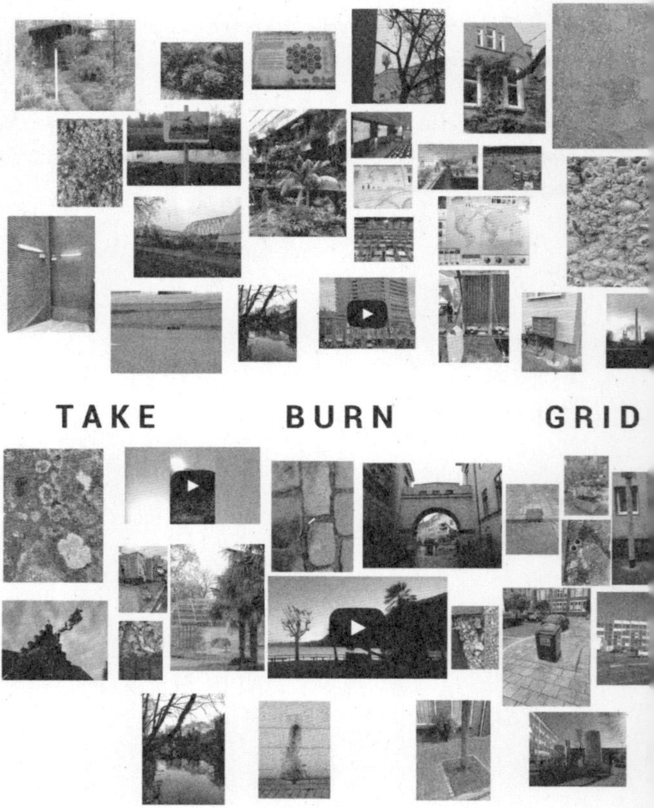
TAKE
BURN
GRID

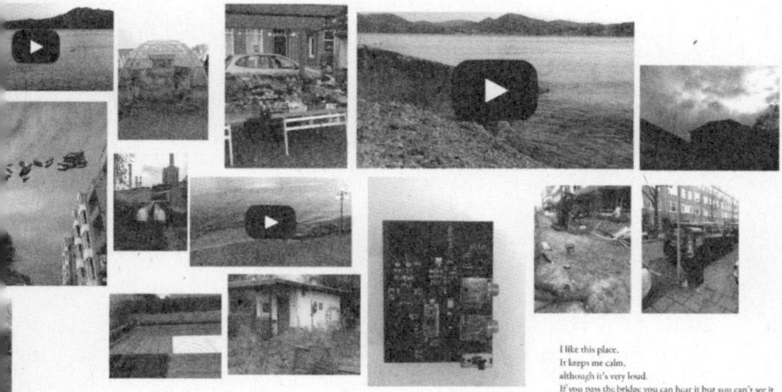

I like this place.
It keeps me calm,
although it's very loud.
If you pass the bridge you can hear it but you can't see it
- and everything stands still.
One day, the sound is gone and I feel sorrow.

SMOOTH & SPEED

ROWD

PIPE

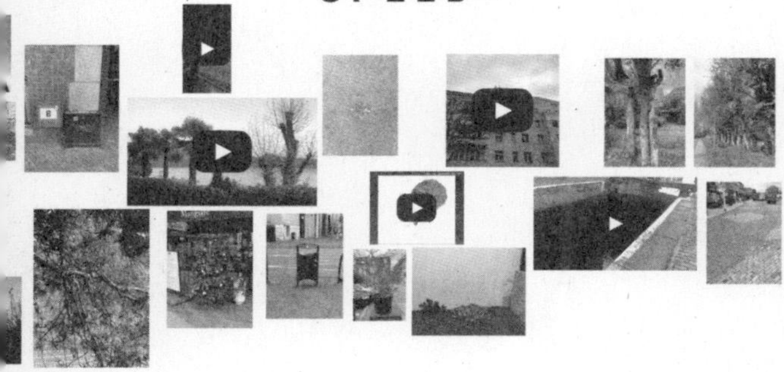

A collective work by the participants of *Feral Atlas as a Verb* at Making Matters Symposium: Collective Material Practices in Critical Times (Het Nieuwe Instituut Rotterdam, 21 Nov 2020) and at Driving the Human Opening Festival (ZKM Karlsruhe, 22 Nov 2020).

return beat

Olu Taiwo

The term *return beat*, as I coined it, refers to a metaphysical experience of West African rhythm that is centered in the body of the performer-participant. The concept of return beat refers to a mode of resonant experience of rhythmic perceptions that is culturally shared and cyclical in nature.

The return beat is transmitted through a praxis I refer to as the Golden Triangle, which uses rhythm as a vehicle that integrates song or spoken word with movement or dance and with percussion or drumming. This integrated triple praxis is then used as a starting point to experience individual and cultural modes of being, becoming, and performance as part of a perception of a plethora of living forces of planet Earth.

Principally, the return beat is a rhythmic paradigm that underpins the embodied knowledge of both Pan African people, in other words people who live on the African continent and people of the Pan African cultural diaspora, who are people of African descent living outside the continent. This embodied knowledge applies a traditional fractal aesthetic in the creation and production of temporal space. This traditional African aesthetic is binary in nature and manifests as endless bifurcations of single pathways. It can be identified in weaving patterns, traditional ornamentation of buildings and utensils, but also in certain images that the mathematician Mandelbrot created to visualize so-called fractals. It observes as well as expresses the continuous twinning process that is required for living bodies to propagate in the world. This aesthetics not only depicts patterns, it also includes the agency of a living body to navigate them, to choose a single pathway in those bifurcating spaces.

return beat and physical journal

Physical journal is a way to conceptualize living bodies from the perspective of a practitioner's lived experience. The physical journal is formed by both genetically and culturally embodied memories that neurologically construct a kind of virtual body, which is holographically projected as our experience of being a lived body. The physical journal is an intertwined set of embodied spatial memories that act as reference frame for living bodies to write and rewrite themselves through experience. It is the spatialized memory of the body itself that acts both as counterpoint for new experiences and as the spatial fabric where these experiences are being inscribed.

The return beat draws attention to the temporal location of the beats as well as the spaces between the beats, as experienced in relation to the physical journal's encounter with the rhythmic flow. The phenomenon of return beat is a specific cultural experience of tempo and its flow within any given rhythm, which is the nature of the beat itself. The resonant embodied understanding of the return beat is experienced as a curve leading back to the individual's sense of self, being, and awareness. By echoing the metabolic circular rhythm of our heartbeat, we create an outgoing (centrifugal) and a returning (centripetal) experience pertaining to the duration between repetitive beats. These beats are perceived to emerge from visceral pathways in our embodied experience.

away from static temporal space

Western temporal-spatial understanding describes repetition as static patterns in duration. This understanding, which neglects the experiencing-performing body and limits itself to repetitive phenomena in a fixed and passive temporal arena, subjugated the Yoruba perspective. It ridiculed the transformative potential of repetition, constraining the understanding of what is rhythmically repetitious and discarding it as unevolved and predictable.

Through this Westerns lens, the concept of a return beat that mobilizes notions of returning to the same experience in distributed regions of time-space, may produce an embodied fear of stagnation. However, if we move away from the disembodied, static perceptions of temporal space—a perceptual hangover from dualism in the Enlightenment—to a more dynamic quantum perception that includes the living body, then repetition does not unfold in stasis but in pulses and waves. Temporal space is then not an empty arena for events to unfold but a substance that contains and yields energy.

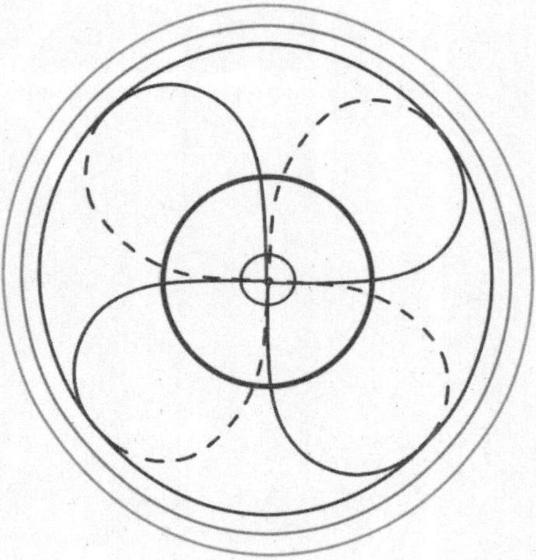

Black lines are the curve flux of experience with the dashed lines representing an outgoing centrifugal experience of the curve flux with the solid line representing the returning centripetal experience. The outer grey concentric circles represent occasions of the unfolding of space time with the centre indicating the location of the return beat.

economy

business

Kate Rich

↦

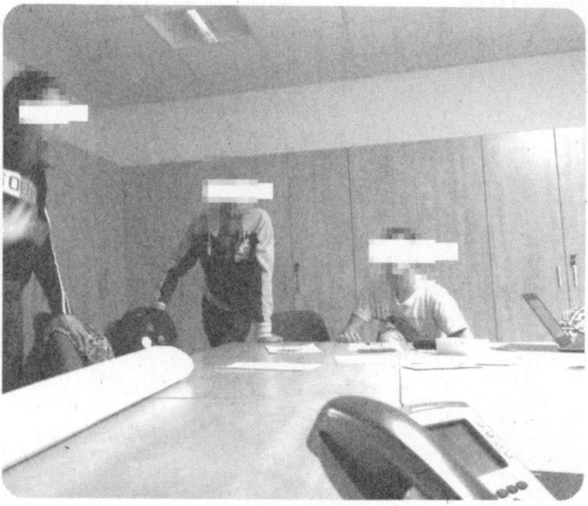

I would like to take up *business* as a term that regularly goes unexamined in the arts and humanities.[1] Yet the idea of business could benefit from further attention, beyond its burnt-out definition of a site where entrepreneurs and workers transform resources into goods and services for profit. Some notions that I have scavenged from the margins of business discourse open up wormholes to new understandings. Management professor Martin Parker calls for an 'insurgent entrepreneurship' that could be critical, experimental, and playful with the economic status quo.[2] Activist lawyer Janelle Orsi asks what would happen if we redefined enterprise as 'any productive activity that could bring us sustenance'?[3] Social innovation scholar Warren Nilsson offers a gravitational vision of 'unbound' organization: an alternative geometry where business 'could have 'a centre but no sides', its activities coordinated through human intentions and relations, not formal structures and agendas.[4] And in the context of critical making↦, social entrepreneur Matthew Manos has speculated on ↦ 'business as a medium for critical inquiry' where the formats and materials of business could be refocused towards meaning-making rather than market-based

1. Try scanning the texts of your favourite philosopher, artist, or activist thinker for business and you might see what I mean.
2. 'Horizons of Possibility: Challenge Co-optation and Transformation', in Martin Parker et al., eds., *The Routledge Companion to Alternative Organization* (London: Routledge, 2013), pp. 359–72.
3. Janelle Orsi, *Practicing Law in the Sharing Economy: Helping People Build Cooperatives, Social Enterprise, and Local Sustainable Economies* (Chicago, IL, American Bar Association, 2012).
4. Warren Nilsson, *Organization Unbound: The Spiritual Architecture of Organizations* (2007). Available at organizationunbound.org/wp-content/uploads/2011/02/Organization-Unbound.pdf.

success.[5] A piñata of possibilities, yet the wider opportunity glimpsed in these statements is that business might not be a done deal, but open to interpretation.

In my own case, I have been working as an artist with business as my medium and material for almost twenty years. My first foray into commerce was with Feral Trade, a sole trader grocery business operating across mixed terrain of art, social networks, and the commodity sphere since 2003 (for a more detailed description, see the entry for feral⇝ in this lexicon). I am also a part of the Cube Cola manufacturing partnership that produces and distributes an open-source cola worldwide. The cola is produced in our kitchen 'lab' and mailed out to customers in concentrate form; the recipe is freely shared. And I am a member of the accounts team at the Cube Microplex in Bristol, an all-volunteer-run arts venue that makes its living from the bar and the door takings. These endeavours are not proudly independent but rather the opposite, they make and maintain their interdependence with a constellation of other enterprises, from corporates to colleagues. These are the waste collectors, the regulatory agencies, the flavour industry giants, but they are also the corner shopkeepers, smallholder farms, feminist server collectives and diy⇝ shipping lines. To mention just a few like-minded endeavours, Company Drinks in London describe themselves as 'art in the shape of a community drinks enterprise'.[6] They run a yearly production cycle making and trading fizzy drinks in

5. Matthew Manos, 'Business as a Medium', in Garnet Hertz, ed., *Critical Making* ([Hollywood]: Telharmonium, 2012), pp. 27–32.
6. Kathrin Böhm and Kuba Szreder, 'How to reclaim the economy using artistic means: The case of Company Drinks', in J.K. Gibson-Graham and Kelly Dombroski, eds., *The Handbook of Diverse Economies* (Cheltenham: Edward Elgar Publishing, 2020), pp. 527–34.

their community, a form of collectivity in art and economy they claim as a new and vital form of public space. And there is the Sail Cargo Alliance, a Europe-wide gathering of wind-powered sailing vessels, ships captains, and cargo brokers who are assembling a grassroots freight system that challenges not only the fuel source but the logic of the whole supply chain, down to what would be traded and why. Critically, these endeavours are not doing art or activism 'about' business but are out there in the world doing business for real.

Taking business as a stage and site for experiments in 'surviving well together' (in the words of feminist economist J.K. Gibson-Graham),[7] the kind that might open up routes into other possible worlds, may seem counter-intuitive. Those working in the arts or education may have experienced being swept up or perhaps dragged under by a tide of business vocabulary and values, encapsulated in the bonanza of the Creative Industries that reconfigures creativity as a driver of economic growth. At the same time, the uneasy covenant that 'business as usual' would maintain a habitable planet has unarguably failed. Yet these fractures and fissures also point to an uncommon potential. business is widely understood and accessible, it operates in and across wildly different collectives, shapes, and scales. It can act as a Trojan horse, an avatar or exoskeleton in which to navigate this hostile yet contestable space that we hazily call 'the economy'. The sail cargo captains are negotiating with commercial harbours to bring their vessels into port alongside the container ships. The artist-led drinks companies are merging their recipes to produce a trans-national cola with the potential to take down a stickily secretive, ↦

7. J.K. Gibson-Graham, Jenny Cameron and Stephen Healy, *Take Back the Economy: An Ethical Guide for Transforming Our Communities* (Minneapolis: University of Minnesota Press, 2013).

world-dominating incumbent. An artist-anarchist farming partnership finds a route through the welfare system to secure the Farm Household Allowance, an income that will bankroll their agriculture experiments for years to come.

In the case of Feral Trade, a few years back I was fortunate enough to be raided by Trading Standards, the UK consumer protection agency. Trading Standards investigates commercial entities that trade outside the law, they have more powers than the police and can for example enter your home without a warrant. They spent hours swarming the Feral Trade website, then cornered me for an interview. After lengthy negotiations, finding no consumer as such to protect—these are peer-to-peer transactions, negotiated entirely through social routes and relations—I received a kind of de facto, state-sanctioned permission to continue trading, in this grey zone of business that Feral Trade has made its home. A tiny island of regulatory indeterminacy, where the relationship between the commercial and the personal is blurred to the point that the law gets a headache.

These are wildly local and contingent examples; they are not models for anything. They are all also imbricated, co-produced and co-dependent with a host of other elements and effects, including the systems they contest. Yet this is also the point. The prospect of business could not be more salient, viewed from the burning debris of a torched economy. We all already are, have, or are in a unit of livelihood, or many—to annex the words of artist Joseph Beuys: 'everyone is a business'! The challenge, and the potential, is to bring our day-to-day subsistence in line with the meanings we want to make. business could be a vehicle for doing that.

recombinant commons

temporary manifesto for a laboratory of recombinant commons

Aliens in Green

↦

re-qualifying the laboratory

Aliens in Green are agents from a planet-turned-laboratory. The laboratory is the place where that which does not yet⇸ exist comes into existence and materializes. On this laboratory-planet, the biosphere has been transformed into a laboratory, affecting what we, species? from the Cenozoic (i.e., the Age of Mammals, from 66 million years ago until today), have known until now.

This future has not yet⇸ been created, but the images coming from it? are materializing in various ways. Some of these images show a xeno-power that elicits the emergence of radically new things and creatures, entities that force the evolution of living beings into divergent paths between species.

In this xeno-laboratory, we are witnessing and anticipating the emergence of systems of our future subordination or extermination based on our own alienation. Against this xeno-laboratory, Aliens in Green position the idea of a non-alien laboratory. This *laboratory commons*, a place where interspecific communities meet and form, continues, rather than breaks with, the community of beings we have experienced throughout the Cenozoic. This laboratory is a place-in-becoming, a place where the combination of living forms, their composition and articulation, is elaborated, a place that the present ruling ontologies would like to curtail.

cultivating an art of combinations

The art of combinations is aimed primarily at recomposing the commons in an odd world. The art of combinations is an art of symbiosis, a common thrust towards *phusis*, or the 'self-giving-of-a-common-form'. Genetic recombination as well as genetic, hormonal, and chemical communication between species is multi-facetted and ongoing. Whereas control over sexual reproduction was part of traditional politics, connecting individuals and populations as well as citizens and states, the non-genealogical and lateral *transfer* of genes, molecules, signals, will perhaps enable us to understand the making of new biological-political connections—between persons and *licenses*, between human and other-than-human user communities, between polymorphisms and policies. These recombinations, which are inherent in society, must emancipate themselves from the specific standards of the bio- and chemo-industrial complex. This is why a critique of xeno-hormones, xeno-molecules, xeno-genes and xeno-(eco- or bio)systems, and a critique of the xeno-powers that define their present and future orientation need to complement a policy of *recombinant commons*.

cultivating an art of composition

↦

A non-anthropomorphic approach to intelligence opens up new spaces of social composition. If we leave behind the anthropomorphic conception of intelligence and acknowledge that intelligence is distributed across all biotic flows, across all plant, animal, fungal, and bacterial species, then social and political compositions will change radically. This post-species-oriented approach reconfigures our modes of operation by aiming to connect the reflexivity and theoretical models inherited from Western anthropoid culture with concrete modes of action generated by other species and flows.

Reflexivity, through its ability to 'render alien' and to create distance, can subvert the process of meaning and enable us to represent the unrepresentable. The non-anthropomorphic approach of affects conversely allows us to rethink the mediations between bodies and signifiers beyond identities and species, and to understand the flow of affects that interconnects and co-constitutes bodies of different kinds.

cultivating an art of articulation

Articulation is a key concept for addressing the *laboratorization* of the living and the capitalist ecosystem, if we do not want to limit our critique to economics and class relations. The concepts of becoming-alien and becoming-non-alien enable us to articulate worlds in a way that neutralizes their potential antagonisms. Their aim is to articulate or coordinate various narratives revealing the anti-terrestrial spirit of capitalism and to create a biospheric commons.

In short, the concepts of becoming-alien and becoming-non-alien allow us to build counter-hegemonic narratives and devices, as well as trans-specific solidarities that are simultaneously political, epistemological, technical, and strategic, and enable anti-systemic struggles to converge.

workshop

Anja Groten

↦

In 2018 my colleague Shailoh Phillips and I organized a *workshop* on 'how to give workshops' at the annual Summer Academy of the Amsterdam-based workshop initiative Hackers & Designers (H&D).[1] The practices of participants joining H&D's activities are usually situated at the intersection of technology, design, and art. H&D's workshops take place in a non-hierarchical manner, meaning that participants become workshop hosts and vice versa. The ways in which the workshop programme unfolds over the course of the Summer Academy is put up for discussion.

Our motivation for hosting⇢ a workshop on how to give a workshop was mostly to pay attention to the format of the workshop itself as it, so far, has remained mostly unquestioned as a format, even though it is a substantial ingredient of H&D's activities. H&D is only one of many similar initiatives that resort to the workshop as a format for organizing events. As an ambiguous format, not tied to a specific context, the workshop crosses many boundaries—between art and activism, between different disciplines and institutions⊕→, between commercial and educational contexts. My attempt at a definition is: a gathering of a committed group of people who want to learn something together in a set time frame. Workshops that I have been part of usually follow a hands-on approach to learning that can be traced back to the Bauhaus. Here, the workshop was the artisan's workplace, a place that bridged the divide between making and thinking, as well as between disciplinary divisions such as sculpting and painting. The workshop brought together art and technology in an attempt to provide solutions for the

1. hackersanddesigners.nl/s/Summer_Academy_2018/p/Work_the_Workshop.

social problems posed by an industrialized, capitalist society.[2]

Workshops like the ones organized at H&D are not bound to any particular space. In this regard they differ from the artisan workshop, which is the site of material production. The workshop does not exclude the possibility for material production or skill transfer and there is a strong incentive to share knowledge and learning experiences through making things. However, making something is not necessarily regarded as a goal. On the contrary, a workshop may become an opportunity to escape the pressure of producing something final or instantaneously useful.[3]

Despite these differences, both the artisan workshop and what I would like to call the 'ephemeral workshop' (as described above) can be seen as social spaces within which material-based learning can take place.

Besides methods, techniques, tools, and protocols, workshops also bring about certain social dynamics that evolve from the particular composition of participants, as well as the context and conditions they find themselves in. Such 'moods' shift and slide and cause particular forms of production and knowledge to emerge, intervene or evaporate. Workshop ↦

2. See Jeroen van den Eijnde, in *Materialization in Art & Design (MAD)*, ed. Herman Verkerk and Maurizio Montalti (London: Sternberg Press, 2019).
3. This non-solutionist approach to workshops cannot be generalized and applied to all contexts where workshops are being used as a format. For instance, workshops conducted in specific activist context cater to transferring concrete skills, and strategies for political action. In her talk 'The Workshop as an Emancipatory Mediation Method of Resistant Practices' the activist Hanna Poddig explained that there is simply not enough time to waste as activists need to teach each other very concretely how to negotiate a confrontation with police in a sit-in for instance, or how to secure yourself when climbing trees in the midst of a forest occupation (in reference to Hambacher Forest protests).

participants and workshop hosts together shape and reshape the dynamic present.

In the 1960s and 1970s the workshop evolved as an extra-curricular self-organized activity that resisted principles of art & design schools such as disciplined and canon-based learning, hierarchies between teachers (instructors) over students (apprentices), as well as the commercialization of workshops to produce 'marketable' goods.

Since the 1990s the workshop format regained traction with a renewed interest in educational experimentation in the arts.[4] Inspired by movements of the 1960s and 1970s such as the 'Free International University',[5] 'Antiuniversity'[6] or the 'Non-School',[7] the so-called educational turn[8] drew attention to collective research, paying attention to processes rather than objects or final outcomes.

Today, collaborative learning, critical pedagogy, and self-organization are still key principles for collective practices that do not abide by the stiff structures of educational and cultural institutions⊕›. Workshops organized today for instance by H&D,[9] Varia,[10] Trojan

4. tate.org.uk/art/art-terms/e/educational-turn.
5. Founded in 1978 by Joseph Beuys in Düsseldorf.
6. The Antiuniversity of London was a short-lived and intense experiment into self-organized education and communal living that took off at 49 Rivington Street in Shoreditch in February 1968. The group included the anti-psychiatrists R.D. Laing and David Cooper; veterans of the Free University of New York; Allen Krebs and Joe Berke; the feminist psychoanalyst Juliet Mitchell; and the cultural theorist Stuart Hall.
7. Founded by Fluxus artists Robert Filliou and George Brecht, in Villefrance (1966).
8. tranzit.org/curatorialdictionary/index.php/dictionary/educational-turn; x-traonline.org/article/rethinking-pedagogical-aesthetics.
9. hackersanddesigners.nl.
10. varia.zone.

Horse,[11] Anhoek School,[12] or Parallel School[13] continue the legacy of ad hoc self-organization, defiant dilettantism, horizontal and collective learning-by-doing.[14]

However, in our day, the workshop has also become a popular genre that functions well within the framework of a service economy. Situated between work and leisure the workshop's commercial potential is explored in the context of conferences, incubator programmes, and creative retreats. Taking place outside of the daily work routine, workshops ought to be fun while valorizing the participants' CV. The workshop has been co-opted by innovation labs and creative agencies and turned into a product itself. For example, *Next Nature*, a speculative design studio, sells

11. trojanhorse.fi.
12. Anhoek School is an experimental all-women's nomadic graduate school. Tuition costs are mediated through a barter system, socialtextjournal.org /periscope_article/anhoek-school.
13. 'Parallel School offers an open environment for self-education in the broader context of art and design. Parallel School belongs to no one. Parallel School has no location. Parallel School is not teaching. Parallel School is learning', parallel-school.org.
14. The goal was not to develop an alternative or other form of institution⊕→ but to remain flexible in a way workshops can be organized. 'Through its process of deinstitutionalization and despecialization "AntiUniversity" shifted from a rather centralized structure to an almost invisible self-organizing anti-anti-university that occurred whenever and wherever. The last trace to be found was a weekend workshop on poetry and philosophy in 1971', in *Contestations: Learning From Critical Experiments in Education*, ed. Tom Vandeputte and Tim Ivison (London: Bedford Press, 2020).

a workshop-in-a-box.[15] Here, the workshop takes on the format of a card game and is described as a '2-hour dynamic crash course [that] helps you to better understand and discuss technology'.[16] It might not be intended as such, but in my view this workshop-in-a-box could be read as a satire on workshops, as an ironic commentary on compulsive self-improvement, learning-by-doing and the pressure to participate in one workshop after the other. The implication of presenting a workshop as a product is that the workshop in and of itself is a highly productive format. What a product like the workshop-in-a-box lacks to address is the unpredictability of a workshop context. Workshop moods that are essential to any workshop experience cannot be predetermined thus, cannot be turned into generic instructions that fit on a card.

In my experiencing there is no such thing as a guarantee for 'a perfect workshop'. Workshop chatter and workshop moods—either friendly and warm or grouchy and agitated—are core ingredients of a workshop situation, but hardly predictable. Still, I do believe that the workshop can be a meaningful tool. The workshop brings about temporary learning environments, in which making processes but also modes of being together are put up for discussion. Workshop situations have challenged me in my lack of patience or my assumptions of what I regarded as productive or efficient. A workshop cannot be taken for granted or defined as a given format or medium, and therefore cannot guarantee any outcome. The

15. 'Are you working on projects where technology and human interaction are involved, and are you looking for a new approach? As of today, we offer a brand-new workshop concept for you and your team. In just two hours you learn how to work with the Pyramid of Technology toolbox in an active, dynamic and 100% analogue way!', nextnature.net/story/2018/next-nature-academy-workshop.
16. Ibid.

workshop comes with the potential for confrontation as much as it can lead to long-lasting collaborations and friendships. A workshop situation may produce disruptions and reciprocal challenging of assumptions engrained in disciplinary habits of how we are practicing. Specific moments of transformation are evoked by making things together, in the 'here and now'.

↦

zoönomy

Klaas Kuitenbrouwer

⟼

Photo: Patricia de Ruijter – mediakaal.nl.

Zoönomy is a proposal for an alternative to capitalist economy and an antithesis to any mode of thought according to which economy is capitalist by definition. The term was coined to address something that does not yet↬ exist, but needs to come into existence: a regenerative economy. But as long as this not-yet↬-existing thing is portrayed as an economy, it will carry forward the sad genealogy of that word since the invention of mercantilism. Zoönomy intends to free 'economy' of its extractivist premises, both in language and in material practices↣.

Zoönomy makes no fundamental distinction between a human economy and economies of other-than-human life. It sidesteps the near-fatal historical mistake of separating human and other-than-human existence. Zoönomy deals with networks of exchange of matter, energy, and meaning that sustain bodies of any kind.

Human economic activity should be reconsidered and transformed into a functioning, supportive zone of a larger zoönomy. Consequently, it would no longer be capitalist. Zoöps⇛ are a testing ground for putting zoönomy into practice. ↦

The practice of zoönomy starts on the inside of late-capitalism (as an outside presently only exists in theory). At the same time, it conceptually surrounds and exceeds the latter's notion of economy by paying qualitative attention to detail, to movement, to beauty, to violence, in short, to other things than quantity and currency.

Zoönomy aims to address the poverty of the capitalist logic, i.e., its metaphysics of one-dimensional quantification. But the issue is not economy per se. Zoönomy includes material exchanges. Like economy in its predominant understanding, zoönomy is a sphere of value. Contrary to mainstream economy, its concept of value cannot be reduced to single, quantifiable, abstracted commodities. Zoönomic value is rooted in a multiplicity of life-worlds, in notions and experiences of variety and richness in relations. Zoönomic understanding is about qualities of relation and form and pattern, aided by quantity only where relevant.

Zoönomic understanding does not operate from a preconceived distinction between physical, material exchange on the one hand and informational or symbolic exchange on the other. In other words, it is not performing any categorical distinction between theory and practice. Zoönomic knowledge lives in all semiotic hot zones: in the indexical exchanges of hormones and chemistry, in the iconic exchanges of empathy across bodies and species, and in the symbolic exchanges of stories and aggregated, distilled experience that, as it turns out, is not an exclusively human practice either.[1]

There is not even a potential end state for the evolution of zoönomic knowledge, as it needs to work from the perspectives of ever more, always different bodies. By this principle, zoönomy is and will have to remain stubbornly open to widely divergent knowledge practices, including those from other-than-human life-worlds, whose realms of existence may only be accessible to human bodies' experience by way of extended metaphor.[2] (And who is to deny the vital role of metaphor in knowledge practices?[3])

1. Eduardo Kohn, *How Forests Think: Toward an Anthropology beyond the Human* (Berkeley: University of California Press, 2013), pp. 38–42; and Eva Meijer, *When Animals Speak, Towards and Interspecies Democracy* (New York: New York University Press, 2019).
2. Ian Bogost, *Alien Phenomenology or What It's Like to Be a Thing?* (Minneapolis: University of Minnesota Press, 2012), pp. 61–84.
3. George Lakoff, *Women, Fire and Dangerous Things* (Chicago: University of Chicago Press, 1987).

The reason we need zoönomy is that under the pervasive semantics of capitalist economy, bodies are only informed by financial signs, designating capitalism's poverty. In opposition, the zoönomy of a place includes its material, thermodynamic, and trophic relations, it includes exchanges of materials and energy, it includes symbolic, aesthetic exchanges: the various ways in which bodies inform and impress each other; how that which can be exchanged, translates from some bodies to some other bodies.

The practice of zoönomy requires that all those proliferating relations are not separated from each other by jargons or institutional traditions, but are perceived and treated as part of the same ontologically flattened, but otherwise exuberantly multidimensional sphere. This means that zoönomy as a knowledge practice hybridizes (conceptual) tools, lenses, ways of doing—from ecology, thermodynamics, economy, cultural analysis, political science, the arts, design, indigenous cosmologies and practices, various older and more recent technologies—hell, even quantum physics! And not in any particular order. ↦

The aim of zoönomy is to develop knowledge practice of bodies that are always collective bodies⇢. Applying zoönomic tools and methods, these bodies will perform[4] a local, distinguishable zoönomy. This zoönomy is both a network of actants, with no clear centre or border,[5] as well as a finite volume, a sphere.[6] Diverse bodies are enrolled in constituting a locally situated zoönomy. This zoönomy is not yet all-inclusive,

4. Kara Barad, 'Posthuman Performativity: Toward an Understanding of How Matter Comes to Matter', *Signs Journal of Women in Culture and Society* 28, no. 3 (2003), pp. 801–31.
5. Bruno Latour, 'Some Experiments in Arts and Politics', *e-flux journal* 23 (March 2011).
6. Ibid.

it still has an inside and an outside. After all, we have to start somewhere.

Zoönomic knowledge is developed and aggregated in response to particular, motivated curiosities of certain collective bodies⇢. Calling this knowledge an effect of curiosity is to say that there is no talk here of a grand theory of zoönomy. There may never be such a theory and certainly not in what is understood as 'theory' today. Zoönomy faces its questions in the field and in the flesh, where there are always open windows, ground fog, creaking hinges and funny smells, membranes, hair roots.

Zoönomy not only has no grand theory, it also does not have a language of its own yet, although it for sure has a liking for biological metaphor. Best we can say is that at the moment, it is in a state of critical *making do* —an ontological pidgin. The first actual Zoöps⇛ that will speak this pidgin, will grow it into a proud creole.

The concept, the practice and the language of zoönomy always have some particular task and are being shaped by performing this task. This task is always situated[7]—it is always a task, an urgency at hand in one or the other Zoöp⇛. The knowledge practice of zoönomy should be capable of adapting to this task at hand, while increasing its integrity, like bone, like nervous tissue. The work is to make it work.

The practice of zoönomy fosters ecological integrity of multispecies communities, of collective bodies⇢. The practice starts with Zoöps⇛ and their surroundings, and from there intends to spread, like a beneficial pandemic, across planet Earth.

7. Donna Haraway, 'Situated Knowledges: The Science Question in Feminism and the Privilege of Partial Perspectives', *Feminist Studies* 14, no. 3 (Autumn, 1988), pp. 575–99.

making

artistic research

Janneke Wesseling

history

Artistic research is a major buzzword in the European art field, in education (art academies and universities) as well as in exhibition circuits (museums, galleries, and biennales). The artist as researcher has become a commonly accepted figure, but was hardly known in the field of contemporary visual art some twenty years ago.

Recent as the phenomenon may be, its roots can be traced back to early twentieth-century art movements such as Surrealism (Bureau de recherches surréalistes founded in 1925 by André Breton) and Marcel Duchamp, and especially to the 1960s and 1970s. Artistic research in visual art is highly indebted to conceptual art as it manifested itself both in the US (Dan Graham, John Baldessari, Hans Haacke, Joseph Kosuth, to mention just a few) and in Europe (George Brecht, Marcel Broodthaers, Hanne Darboven). In conceptual art, theoretical reflection plays a pivotal role. According to the early conceptual artists, the art work cannot not be separated from the context of history and politics and in order to produce art it was regarded as essential for artists to politically and discursively engage with society. Not only did conceptual artists reflect on societal and political issues, but on art and the art practice itself. They regarded critical reflection on one's artistic procedures or doings as essential to the artistic process or *as* the artistic process itself. Language and text therefore acquired an important role in art practice and writings could be part of the art work or even constitute the work itself (such as in the case of Robert Barry, Kosuth and the early work of Lawrence Weiner).

Another important factor in the emergence of theory and criticism as artistic practice were feminist art practices that aimed to reveal power structures and patterns of hierarchy in society and in the art world (Elaine Sturtevant, Louise Lawler, Jenny Holzer, Barbara Kruger).

For present-day artists, to position themselves as researcher rather than as a producer of marketable goods offers an alternative to the dominance of economic liberalism in the art field and to the capitalist exploitation that is tied to the production of goods. The artist-as-researcher problematizes, contextualizes, and re-enacts social, political, and environmental issues.

terminology

Artistic research could simply be defined as research carried out by artists (designers, composers, choreographers etc.)[1] It is practice-based research that is carried out in and through artistic practice.[2]

In artistic research, practical action (making) and theoretical reflection (thinking) go hand-in-hand, action and thought are inextricably linked. This type of research does not have a predetermined methodology. Like art practice, each artistic research project is idiosyncratic by nature, determined by the desire of the researcher to reflect on their practice, in collaboration with others.[3] The artistic researcher works through theory-practice entanglements. This is to say, not by using practice as an illustration of theory

1. I use 'art' here in an inclusive way, encompassing all artistic disciplines.
2. Generally, in the Anglo-Saxon countries the term 'practice-based' or 'practice-led' research is used. Because of the traditionally subordinate status of 'practice' in the humanities, in European countries the term 'artistic research' is preferred.
3. phdarts.eu.

or vice versa, but by exploring ways in which theory and practice are mutually implicated.[4]

Of course, art by its very nature is intelligent and cognitive: art practice aims to gain a better understanding of the world and to deliver new perspectives on reality. In this broad sense, for many centuries, beginning with Leonardo da Vinci and the Renaissance, research has been recognized as part of the work artists were doing. In our time, that is since the twentieth century, a large part of contemporary art production can, at least to some degree, be identified with critical (self-)reflection (as argued above). So, if research is a natural part of art practice, 'innate' to it, then why would we want to use the term 'research' at all when we speak about art? What does it add? Art in itself is not in need of the qualification of 'research'. Artists are in no way required to demonstrate that they are doing research, neither are they required to account for or explicate what they are doing and how they are doing it.

In an academic context, artistic research has acquired a more specific, and perhaps more relevant, meaning. As a consequence of the so-called Bologna Agreements (1999),[5] entailing a Europe-wide reorganization of education which aimed at establishing a comparable BA and MA framework for all European countries, it became possible for artists and artistic 'makers' to obtain the PhD degree. Here, doing research means referring to making a particular research project that is made public *as research project*, including the artistic process that underlies it. In this context, certain criteria will have to be fulfilled. Such as the requirement that the researcher seeks

4. Petra Klusmeyer, *Sonic Periferies*, PhD dissertation, Leiden University, 2019, p. 31.
5. ec.europa.eu/education/policies/higher-education/bologna-process-and-european-higher-education-area, accessed 14 December 2021.

the discussion in the public domain. The artist-as-researcher distinguishes herself from other artists by taking it upon herself to gain a deeper understanding of the production of the work and the thinking process through a continuous dialogue with others. The artist-researcher allows others (peers, colleagues) to participate in their creative process, entering into a discussion with them and opening herself up to critique. In this context, the public dimension of research, in the sense of making the artistic process public and explicating the so-called 'tacit knowledge' embodied in the work and the practice, is at its core.

critical making

Florian Cramer

On its most simple level, *critical making* is a contraction of 'making' and 'critical thinking'.[1] According to its inventor Matt Ratto, critical making 'signals a desire to theoretically and pragmatically connect two modes of engagement with the world that are often held separate—critical thinking, typically understood as conceptually and linguistically based, and physical 'making,' goal-based material work'.[2] Critical making thus fuses theory and practice, idea and matter; domains that were traditionally separated in Western culture (material practice↣).

Critical making has a cultural and material affinity to maker culture and simple-to-use digital technologies (such as Open Source software, social media and 3D printing) that are thought to foster a culture of 'diy⇝ citizenship'.[3] In critical making, these technologies are not only used to bridge thinking and making, but also to introduce elements of design education into social sciences at universities.

Critical making knows at least three different definitions and schools:

1. critical making developed and practiced in and for social sciences at the University of Toronto by Matt Ratto and his research team;
2. critical making as socially engaged maker culture, practiced by Garnet Hertz and his research team at Emily Carr University in Vancouver;
3. critical making as a design ethos, proposed and practiced among others at the Rhode Island School of Design.

1. Hertz, 'Two Terms.'
2. Ratto, 'Critical Making', p. 254.
3. Ratto and Boler, *DIY Citizenship*.

critical making in social sciences

The following is based on information provided by ginger coons, who completed her PhD research in the critical making Lab of University of Toronto:

critical making, in this school, is a practical study and research method for students and scholars with no art, design or engineering background to do part of their classroom study through material experimentation instead of only reading and discussing texts.

Open Source and Internet 'maker' technologies dramatically lower the threshold for non-experts to build something—an object, a piece of technology, an application—to serve as a temporary, experimental, and discursive device for studying and exploring a concept or theory.

A cultural studies or feminist theory class, for example, could use critical making as a classroom method to study and discuss the claim of the African American poet and critic Audre Lorde that 'The Master's Tools Will Never Dismantle the Master's House',[4] by practically experimenting with the possibilities and limitations of using corporate social media platforms⇛ such as YouTube and Instagram for anti-corporation political activism.

critical making as socially engaged maker culture

'Maker spaces' became a mainstream phenomenon with the creation of the first 'Fab[rication] Lab' at the Massachusetts Institute of Technology in 2001 and the launch of *Make:* magazine in 2005 with its network of over two hundred licensed 'Maker Faire' conventions

4. Lorde, *The Master's Tools Will Never Dismantle the Master's House.*

in more than forty countries. From the perspective of digital media artists, 'maker culture' boiled down to a mainstreaming and commercialization of radical technological diy⇝ that had existed from Nam June Paik's self-constructed video synthesizer in the 1960s to, among others, artists' experiments with self-built radio and tv infrastructures in the 1970s and 1980s, and the 'tactical media' movement of the 1990s.

This difference in politics is epitomized by a cover of *Make:* magazine (vol. 25, 2011) and its parody, *Made:* by the designer and artist Garnet Hertz (2012):

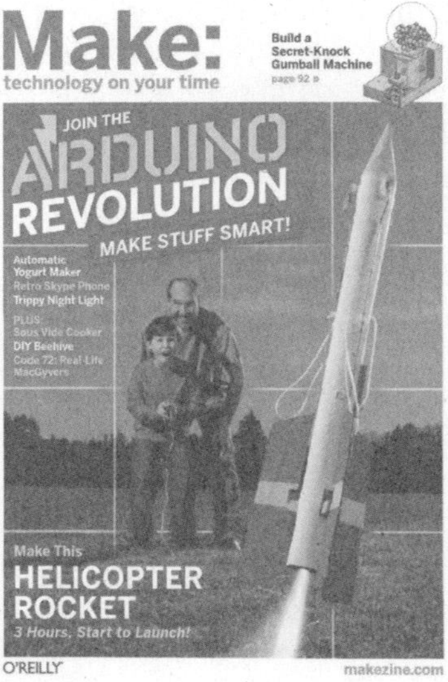

Make: magazine, vol. 25, O'Reilly Publishers, 2011.

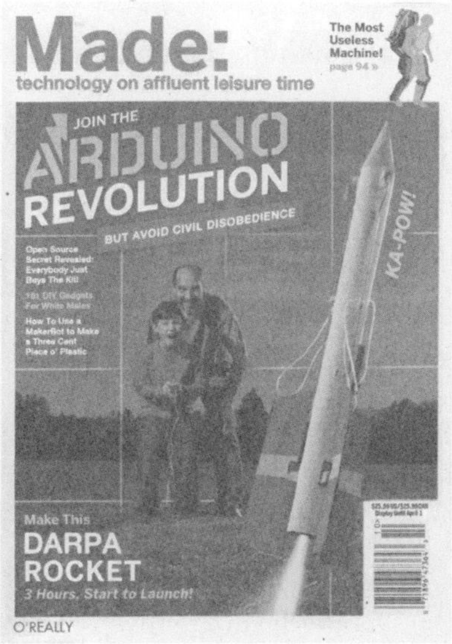

Made: (parody of *Make:* magazine), Garnet Hertz, 2012.

In a series of freely distributed and freely downloadable critical making zines, Hertz positions critical making as an umbrella term for any art and design practice that experiments with technology in critical or non-mainstream ways: from the post-punk robotics of the 1980s Californian Survival Research Labs collective to 'tactical media' art like the political graffiti-spraying robots of the Institute of Applied Autonomy, the 'critical engineering' of the homonymous collective around Danja Vasiliev and Julian Oliver, to the *critical design* of Anthony Dunne and Fiona Raby (which Ratto differentiates from his own concept of critical making).

critical making as a design ethos

Design educators often fail to see a difference between critical making and design education as it has been practiced in art schools for many decades, since design classes often involve concepts from critical theory explored in material projects. In Ratto's concept of critical making, however, objects made by students are not design projects, but merely makeshift devices that are discarded at the end of the class. The difference is similar to that between a social science class where concepts are temporarily visualized with drawings on a blackboard to an art class where students' drawings are the end product.

Since Ratto nevertheless brings 'making' into university classrooms, it is not surprising that design educators conversely reclaim critical making for their own practice, in the broadest sense of the term. An example of this is the 2013 book *The Art of Critical Making* by the Rhode Island School of Design in which the school refers to its entire curriculum as critical making.

epilogue

In 2019, a bankruptcy of *Make:* magazine marked an end of over-optimistic expectations for maker culture. Still, the term 'maker culture' has stuck and makes it difficult to use critical making for practices outside or beyond maker spaces.

references

Bogers, Loes and Letizia Chiappini, eds. *The Critical Makers Reader.* INC Reader 12. Amsterdam: Institute of Network Cultures, 2019, research.hva.nl/en/publications/fe892f5e-c7b9-4a1a-9b76-1674562d56f0.

Hertz, Garnet. *Critical Making.* Vancouver: Telharmonium, 2012.

Hertz, Garnet. 'Two Terms: Critical Making + D.I.Y.' *conceptlab.com*, 2020. conceptlab.com/2terms/pdf/hertz-2terms-202011181901.pdf.

Lorde, Audre. *The Master's Tools Will Never Dismantle the Master's House.* London: Penguin, 2018.

Maeda, John. *The Art of Critical Making: Rhode Island School of Design on Creative Practice.* Edited by Rosanne Somerson and Mara Hermano. Hoboken, New Jersey: Wiley, 2013.

Ratto, Matt. 'Critical Making: Conceptual and Material Studies in Technology and Social Life.' *The Information Society* 27, no. 4 (2011), pp. 252–60.

Ratto, Matt, and Megan Boler, eds. *DIY Citizenship: Critical Making and Social Media.* Cambridge, MA: MIT Press, 2014.

→

destruction

Dani Ploeger

→

Industrial destruction of unused, 'off-spec' products at Northeast Data Destruction, Mansfield, MA.

At first sight, acts of material *destruction* often seem to take place outside the aura of newness that permeates the everyday and its representations⊕→ in consumer culture. However, a closer look shows that, as a matter of fact, destructive processes are at the core of capitalist culture. Drawing from Marx, economist Joseph Schumpeter suggests that capitalist economies are driven by what he calls the 'gale of creative destruction'.[1] In order to generate new surplus value, the capitalist economic system requires a continuous process of destroying existing structures. This happens on a systemic level, as the continuous reshaping of economic orders, but also in immediate material confrontations of war, demolition, and wilful neglect. Demolishing old buildings and infrastructures is oftentimes promoted because it 'creates jobs' and the engineering of 'planned obsolescence' in commodities can be seen as the design of processes of auto-destruction.

In everyday life, the practices of destruction that constitute the 'back end' of liberal capitalism are covered up by an incessant stream of representations⊕→ of the smooth, the shiny, and the new. The weapon trade fair may be the most radical manifestation of this dialectic. While the majority of commodities offered here are unambiguously conceived to enact material destruction, their modes of representation⊕→ as a rule exceed the visual languages of consumerism in terms of the prominence of clean and spotless, slick material surfaces.

Schumpeter's 'gale of creative destruction' can be seen as part of a broader characteristic of capitalist expansionism. In *A History of the World in Seven Cheap Things*, Raj Patel and Jason W. Moore argue that capitalist enterprise is underpinned by a never-ending

1. J.A. Schumpeter, *Capitalism, Socialism and Democracy* (London: Routledge, 1994 [1942]).

drive towards accessing ever cheaper resources in the form of nature, money, work, care, food, energy, and lives.[2] In the context of this process of endless cheapening, 'creative destruction' operates as a catalyst for the system's incessant need for devaluation. As such, the destructive tendency that lies at the core of capitalist enterprise contributes to its character as essentially a 'frontier technology' that in its search for cheapness is in a very fundamental way irreconcilable with ambitions to establish a truly ecologically sustainable economic model.

There are also forms of destruction that exist beyond the logic of Schumpeter's 'gale of creative destruction'. Destruction caused by natural, non-human phenomena may nowadays occur as an indirect result of extractivist economic activity and will often quickly be subsumed in a process of commodification where ecological disaster serves as a cue for the development of new products, as is the case in e.g., the export of Dutch engineering systems to counter the threats of rising sea-levels in Jakarta, Indonesia.[3] Nevertheless, these forms of destruction that are not directly anthropogenic also fall outside the sphere of human control and are posing fundamental systemic challenges. Climate-change induced natural destruction will drastically limit access to cheap resources on a global scale. At some point the final

2. R. Patel and J.W. Moore, *A History of the World in Seven Cheap Things* (Berkeley: University of California Press, 2017).
3. In the so-called 'Master Plan for the National Capital Integrated Coastal Development' (NCICD) which was drawn up by a consortium of Dutch engineering and consultancy companies, entrepreneurial interests seem to clearly prevail over social and ecological interests. M. Bakker, S. Kishimoto and C. Nooy, *Social Justice at Bay: The Dutch Role in Jakarta's Coastal Defence and Land Reclamation* (Amsterdam: Both ENDS; SOMO; TNI, 2017), available at: www.tni.org/my/node/23480, accessed 22 December 2021.

frontier in the ceaseless quest towards cheapness will be reached.

In addition to destruction caused by natural, non-human phenomena, there is also direct, human induced destruction that takes place outside—and in opposition to—the 'gale of creative destruction'. Through acts of unmaking↬, the mechanisms of capitalist production and consumption may be sabotaged to promote interests beyond mere cheapening and surplus value optimization.

↬

queering (x) making

Z. Blace

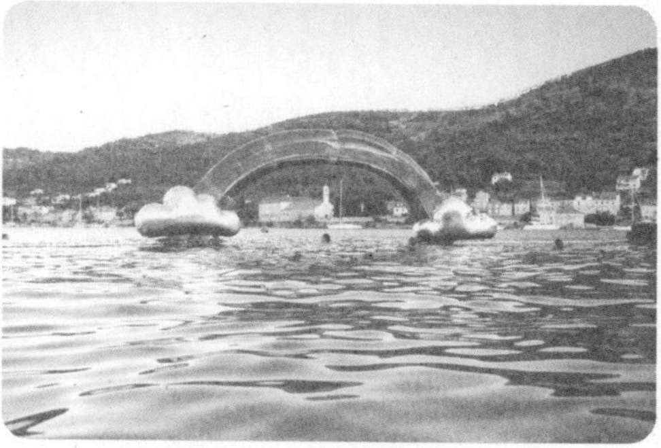

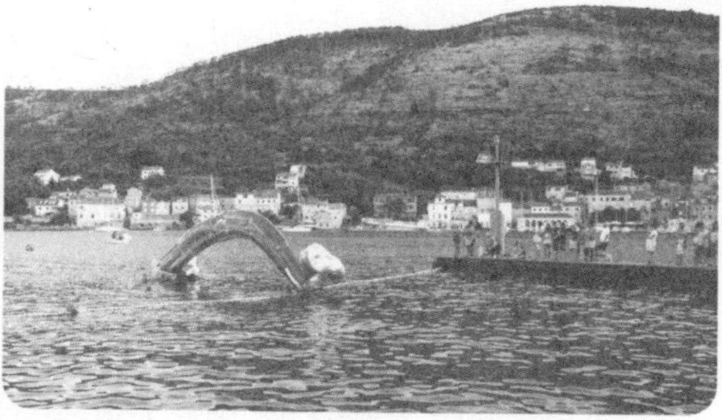

Pop-up RAINBOW making workshops and action conducted by Artúr van Balen and Z. Blace (of ToolsForAction.net and QueerSport.info) with LGBTIQ and Green Action activists at MaMa club Zagreb, and with queer and feminist activists in LGBT Centre Split and at multiple locations on the Island of Vis, Croatia, 2014.

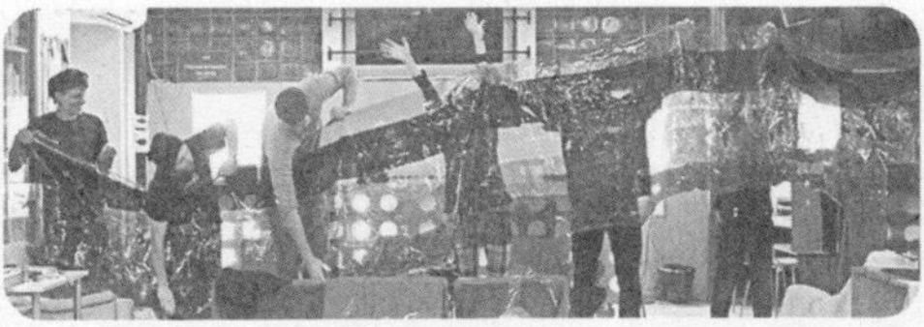

Team Rainbow, 2014.

X

Queering (x) making aspires to situate and communize the concept of (critical) making↬, through focusing on social and cultural urgencies that exceed (merely) material practices↣. It puts (critical) making↬ into different contexts/realities, introducing it to diverse non-normative/vulnerable social groups and individuals. Through creating messy (and sticky) relations between conditions, (co-)creation, criticality⊕→, context and constituents, it discloses and dismantles both the underlying 'productive' norms and norm-ing of mainstream cultural and societal fabrications, as well as those of relatively privileged (academic and artistic) production. It instigates, informs, and inspires interventions by those who are (in most cases) denied access to means of production, overlooked in calculations of consumption, and excluded from long-term reflections and imaginations of diy⇝. ↬

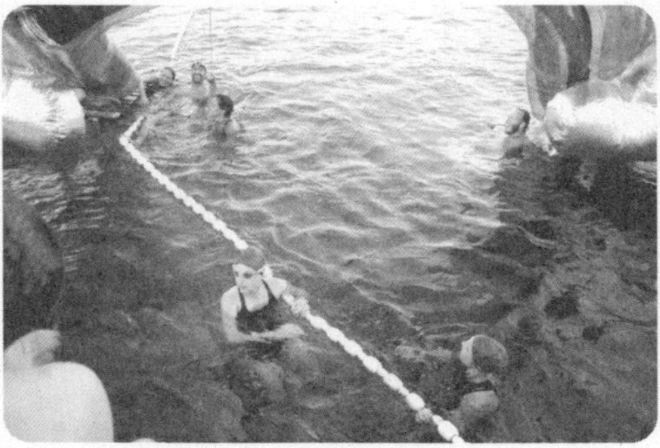

Swimming Marathon in Vis, August 2014,
by Csilla Hódi for Tools for Action and QueerSport.

scoring

Lilia Mestre – a.pass

In the context of a.pass, I have developed an approach to using scores as a pedagogical tool, titled Scorescapes, following the institutional desire for instigating co-learning through making and criticality⊕↛.

Our score practice consists of weekly encounters with a group of artistic researchers↬. It frames the time and space for task-oriented encounters on a regular basis, as a form of conversation and exchange. These meetings are based on a Q-and-A structure that entails material practices↣ and the formulation of questions.

1. Each participant in the score practice presents, in the first meeting, their work in a chosen medium for five minutes.
2. A procedure of changing roles assigns a person to formulate reflections and questions to another person: by chance operation, it's assigned who formulates reflections and questions to whom.
3. Reflections and questions are shared by the participants by email with a delay of two days.
4. The responses are presented in five-minute presentations the week after.
5. The full process is repeated weekly for a period of three months.

INSTRUCTIONS:

- 1 -

Score sessions are organized on a weekly basis.

- 2 -

Participants come together to discuss their case, work process and interests following the block programme.

- 3 -

Before the end of each session we assign the interviewer and interviewee for the following week. A Google document is then created with the number of the session and the names of the participants.

- 4 -

Each participant asks a question by e-mail (and copy-pastes her/his answer on the weekly Google document) to one of the other participants.

- 5 -

Take a maximum of two days to ask your question so the person has at least four days to respond before the next session.

- 6 -

Each participant answers by e-mail and copy-pastes her/his answer on the weekly Google document within the following four days.

- 7 -

If you want to join the score, formulate a question and answer it yourself. Join the meeting to read your question and answer.

- 8 -

We do not read answers if the writers are not present. If you miss a session, you can join in with your last question/answer in a later session.

- 9 -

Reading the answers is the collective core of the system and the generator of new questions.

From: Lilia Mestre and Elke Van Campenhout, eds., *Writing Scores*, (Brussels: a.pass, 2014).

The focal point of using scores (i.e., sets of instructions like the one above) as a pedagogical tool is to bring together a plurality of practices in conversation, without determining the languages these practices are 'talking'—movement, words, text, somatic approaches, film, design, activism, theory. The participants of the score contribute to each session with materials that engage their concepts, forms, and contents as performative contributions to collective learning. The [often unexpected] subjective positions emerging from these encounters are produced by the way proposals are materialized, addressed, and situated.

Who's talking through them, who are they talking to, and what kind of entanglements are they proposing?

The score can be seen as a generative infrastructure that invites to participate as fellow researchers in each other's practice. It is a form of engaged spectatorship based on responsiveness and response-ability (K. Barad) which allows to think through the relations and attachments suggested in each participant's proposal.

Because it is a formalist tool, the score works as a perverse partner that regulates mutual relations and modes of presence through chance procedures, enabling connections that otherwise would maybe not be experienced. It is useful to think of the score as a self-regulating infrastructure operating through people's practices and contents. This practice asks for attendance in a state of shared alertness for the individual and collective assemblages, entanglements and situatednesses that the research practices of the participants propose. The paradox between the formal precision of the score and the unpredictability of the materials that are produced, allows for the experience of aesthetic and ethical readings that reconsider and reposition oneself as part of world(s).

In trying to deal with questions related to co-learning that aim to encompass dissensus, not knowing, methodological understanding, authorship, politics, backgrounds, histories, criticality⊕›, sociability, institutional framework, philosophy, ecologies, and material practice↣ (a lot!), the scores can enable a platform⇛ for exchange through critical making↬.

What we can learn from engaging with each other in such a way, is that form and content are always already symptomatic of a set of relations, and that these sets of relations propose degrees of inclusiveness, contradictions, and resistance. The venture of this kind of proposition is to support articulation of artistic practices as fundamentally relational, embedded and potentially critical to forms of governance (because it is itself of form of governance that makes participants aware of the arbitrary character of rules). The subjectivities that become manifest in the *scoring* practice can be seen as organisms who gain sustainability and stability through their interplay and gradually improving cohabitation. Score, in this way, becomes a constructed framework through which an ecology of practices (Isabelle Stengers) is manifested, each of them revealing their support structure and proliferating within the alliances, conflicts, and proximities they evoke. ↬

These encounters propose a form of sociability, by their regular character over a period of time, but most of all by virtue of the subjectivities that emerge out of them. The type of engagement at stake is one that I can name as friendship (see artificial friendship⇛): curiosity, presence, offering of time, attention, staying with, consideration, but also dissensus, opposition and criticality-⊕→ as a form of care.

The question these scores address and that I'm eager to expand and discuss would be how to develop infrastructures that frame, without polarizing or stigmatizing, knowledge production; how to think infrastructures of encounter that propose ways of 'reading' and 'writing', 're-reading' and 're-writing' through each other's practice, as a methodology for understanding and crafting differences that matter outside of specialization or a discipline. What kinds of institutional support structures can be developed to sustain and empower the transformation and re-actualization of the values attached to artistic practice, and how to value them as matters of concern? (Bruno Latour)

The eternal quest for understanding, and the eternal impossibility of achieving it, leaves us with the wonderful possibility to experience/experiment with complexities.

the not-yet

Frans-Willem Korsten

The not-yet is an intentionally anti-utopian attitude and mode of practice that anticipates future developments by realizing the potential in and of the 'now'. As philosopher Hans Achterhuis noted, all utopian projects in a sense reject the present, or consider it as something to be destroyed in order to make way for the new.[1] The not-yet, instead, suggests that a future is already here, as a potential to be found and cared for.

It considers 'an effort to collectively inhabit alternative imaginaries'. Instead of destroying the present, it aims to interrupt present conditions in order to *learn*.[2] If anything, the not-yet is a matter of a 'transformative practice'.

1. making a case for an alternative future

What potentials does a practice of the not-yet have? How can art's critical potential be used to explore alternative possibilities in the present that materialize in a process of learning? The case presented here is a project that taught me a lot. It was called *De vleesvrije stad*, or *The Meat Free City* and materialized in book form, and digitally on the website of Drawing the Times, a 'platform⇒ for graphic journalism' initiated by artist and graphic journalist Eva Hilhorst.[3]

1. Hans Achterhuis, *Utopie* (Amsterdam: Ambo, 2006); *Koning van Utopia: Nieuw licht op het utopisch denken* (Rotterdam: Lemniscaat, 2016).
2. Cf. Jeanne van Heeswijk, Maria Hlavajova and Rachael Rakes, eds., *Toward the Not-yet: Art as Public Practice* (Cambridge, MA: MIT Press, 2021), p. 14.
3. See drawingthetimes.com/specials/the-meat-free-city/.

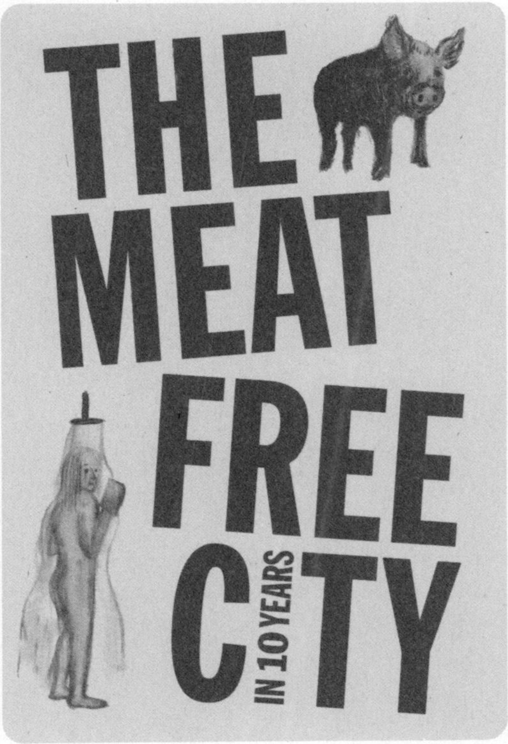

Front cover of the book.

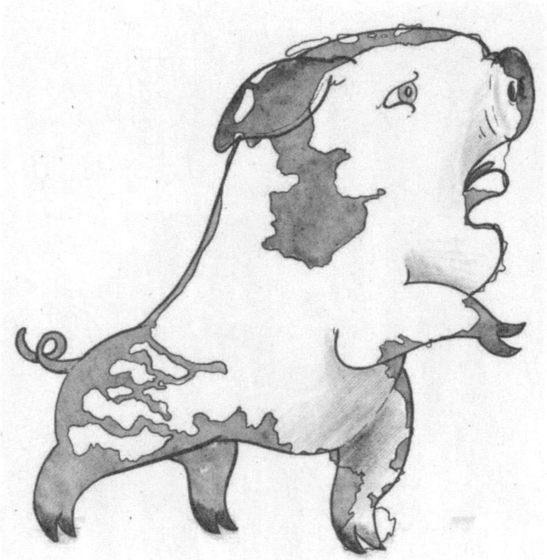

One of the drawings by Merel Barends that shows the Netherlands in the shape of a pig, as an alternative for the well-known Dutch Lion, symbol and icon for the nation; drawingthetimes.com.

The Meat Free City project had its inspiring source in artist-designer Mark Schalken, and became a collective learning process in which all participants—graphic artists, scholars, designers, journalists—discovered potentials in a present that might form the beginnings of another future. Tellingly, the project was subtitled: 'in ten years'. Yet this did not concern a blueprint for a manageable plan with concrete steps to be taken. Rather, the participants were asked to think of possibilities existing in the present and how to hypothetically realize them—at a certain moment in time, and within a time span of ten years. Each contribution focuses on an imaginary year, consequently, in which, for instance, schools host living animals and take them up in the curriculum; supermarkets no longer sell meat; municipal councils give one third of their seats to representatives of different groups of animals (zoöp⇛). Thus, the idea was not just to imagine alternatives but to emphasize that these possibilities are already here, and could as well be realized now.

2. the principle of hope made real

The very phrase 'the not-yet' was coined by Ernst Bloch in an extensive study called *The Principle of Hope*, written between 1938 and 1947. Instead of resorting to the humanist origin of the term utopia as a product of the imagination, Bloch argued that throughout history, utopias have been everywhere, as materializations of hope that do not depend on an imagined alternative or a promise but on something to be *done* in the here and now. In contrast, the Enlightenment utopian/dystopian complex with figures such as the Marquis de Condorcet, depended on a historiography that depicts the process of mankind as progress, as a matter of growing complexity and improvement. The utopian future can be predicted and made top-down, not just as a matter of imagining a better or more beautiful world, but of managing a reality in terms of the probability to get there. The nineteenth century would come to witness what this meant, in the areas of urban planning and landscape design. This, however, paled in comparison to how in the twentieth century entire environments were imagined and built from scratch, and agro-industries and biotechnologies would start to reconfigure the entire idea of life—of all life.

In the project *The Meat Free City*, the hope for an alternative future found an anchor point in a collective process. This made the concept of hope materially real, through a mode of working together in commitment and solidarity. The project started in May 2020, smack in the middle of the Covid isolation, and would result in a publication of a Dutch book plus a digital version in English, in the spring of 2021. When publishers proved to be reluctant to bring out the book, or demanded the right to considerably alter its form and contents, the collective decided to raise money themselves, thus involving even more people but also safeguarding the artistic concept and process. The hope and reality of making this art piece in practice thus came to resonate with the hope and reality of an alternative future.

3. the not-yet as a commitment to the present

When the Meat Free City collective accepted its task of making a work of art that would manifest an alternative reality, they decided to focus on the existing present. Obviously, this did not imply that they accepted everything the present had to offer. In fact, some of the contributors found out that the meat industry was even more abysmal than they had previously thought. For all participants, the project consisted of a collective pedagogical endeavour:

a process of learning together, sharing knowledge, and considering different forms of imagining futures that would do justice to both the present and the future.

In this light, Donna Haraway's *A Cyborg Manifesto* from 1985 still holds its force. In this manifesto, Haraway proposed an alternative future. The distinction between manifesto and utopia is pivotal here, in terms of function, style, and aim. The manifesto provoked its readers not so much to think of possible futures but to conceive of a better future as a possibility in the present. Like Marx and Engels, Haraway insisted 'that possibilities for better worlds are born inside not outside the present relations of domination'.[4] This is why the potential of a collective that Haraway provocatively located in the cyborg is 'fully implicated in the world'.[5] Or, again, instead of fleeing towards the future on the basis of a fictive blueprint, real improvement is only possible if people consciously 'inhabit the despised place'.[6] Or, it is within an existing mode of production where the potential for a better world lingers, not as an ideal but within the material givens of that very world, and in the nigh inexhaustible potential embodied in life as *zoë* (zoöp⇒ and zoönomy↦).

4. Kathi Weeks, 'The Critical Manifesto: Marx and Engels, Haraway, and Utopian Politics', *Utopian Studies* 24, no. 2 (2013), pp. 216–31, p. 225.
5. Donna Haraway, 'A Manifesto for Cyborgs: Science, Technology, and Socialist Feminism in the 1980s', *Socialist Review* 80 (1985), pp. 65–107, p. 95.
6. Donna Haraway, 'Nature, Politics, and Possibilities: A Debate and Discussion with David Harvey and Donna Haraway', *Environment and Planning D: Society and Space* 13 (1995), pp. 507–27, p. 514.

4. conditions of change: interruption or arranging coincidence

In recent years, a popular term in artistic circles was 'intervention'. The term means, literally, that artists 'come in-between', perhaps in order to change a given situation. With the not-yet, however, the focus on both the collective process and the commitment to the present implies that intervention is only viable when artists do not already know what needs to be changed, but intervene to make change possible. Another term introduced in this context is 'interruption', a term that is of special relevance in the context of a capitalist system that can only function on the basis of constant movement; a movement that also blocks the emergence of alternatives. With respect to this, artist Jeanne van Heeswijk, in cooperation with BAK-Utrecht, shifted the emphasis from 'emergency' to 'the emergent' in the project 'Trainings for the Not-yet'.[7] 'The emergent' aimed to underscore the possibilities in the now, or the potential in the present, but also emphasized that the situation must be such that something can indeed emerge. The question then becomes what kinds of practices can make things emerge or coincide, in a process that time and time again asks participants to sense the implications of their practices or what the consequences of their actions may be. This is why the title of the project did not have 'training' in the title but 'trainings': practices. In this context, strategy has to give in to tactics. The tactic to make things coincide is a tactic of arrangements, which can be transformative itself. Or, in working towards such coincidence, training for the not-yet will inevitably imply transforming one's self.

7. See e-flux.com/announcements/266969/trainings-for-the-not-yet/.

unmaking

Dani Ploeger

In the practice of critical making↬, the focus is on the processes of making, rather than on the outcomes of these processes in the form of artefacts. This then forms the basis for critical reflection on creativity, production, and consumption (see criticality⊕↠). If the aim of this critical engagement is to formulate alternatives to the mechanisms and cultural habits of endless accumulation and expansion—the backbone of economic liberalism—we must also consider material processes that take place beyond or in opposition to the making of new artefacts and look towards processes of deterioration and acts of destruction↬. In this, it is important to distinguish between the processes of destruction↬ that are inherent in capitalist expansionism (see destruction↬) and those that destabilize or challenge the systemic status quo. The latter can be designated as acts of *unmaking*.

The study and exploration of these 'outcast' processes and the ways in which—and reasons why— they are excluded from dominant narratives in consumer culture could inform perspectives that challenge the myth of endless growth.

Unmaking may involve breaking technological devices, such as the Luddites' attacks on textile machinery in the early nineteenth century, but it can also concern the creation of technological devices in order to destroy (part of) the domain of production and consumption. Improvised Explosive Devices (IEDs) are an example of this. Such acts and technologies of unmaking are commonly dismissed as nihilistic violence aimed at the supposedly peaceful everyday of consumer culture. However, considering that destruction↬ is actually an essential component of the very logic of capitalism—albeit often hidden below its shiny surfaces—processes of unmaking should rather be examined as transgressions of the inherent destructive violence of the 'business↦ as usual' of production and consumption.

Practices of unmaking can be read in the context of Slavoj Žižek's analysis of the relationship between subjective and objective forms of violence: '... subjective violence is experienced as such against the background of a non-violent zero level. It is seen as a perturbation of the "normal", peaceful state of things. However, objective violence is precisely the violence inherent in this "normal" state of things.'[1]

Acts of unmaking form an explicit response to the often-overlooked objective violence of destruction↬-based economic activity.

As such, unmaking can be experienced as subjective violence from the perspective of regular consumers. However, it should rather be read as a form of unmasking, a pulling away of the shiny surface of consumer culture to bring the inherent violence to light. But in fact, what is indicated with 'unmaking' here, is more than what is captured by the notion of unmasking. It is an affirmative escape from both the opaque glitz of consumer surfaces as well as from the extractivist (i.e., extracting natural resources from the Earth) business↦-as-usual of the larger capitalist machine. Unmaking is to be understood as a combined material, creative and symbolic negation breaking matter away from its looming capitalist burden and making it available for other meanings, other ↬ appropriations, other play.

1. Slavoj Žižek, *Violence: Six Sideways Reflections* (London: Profile Books, 2008), p. 2.

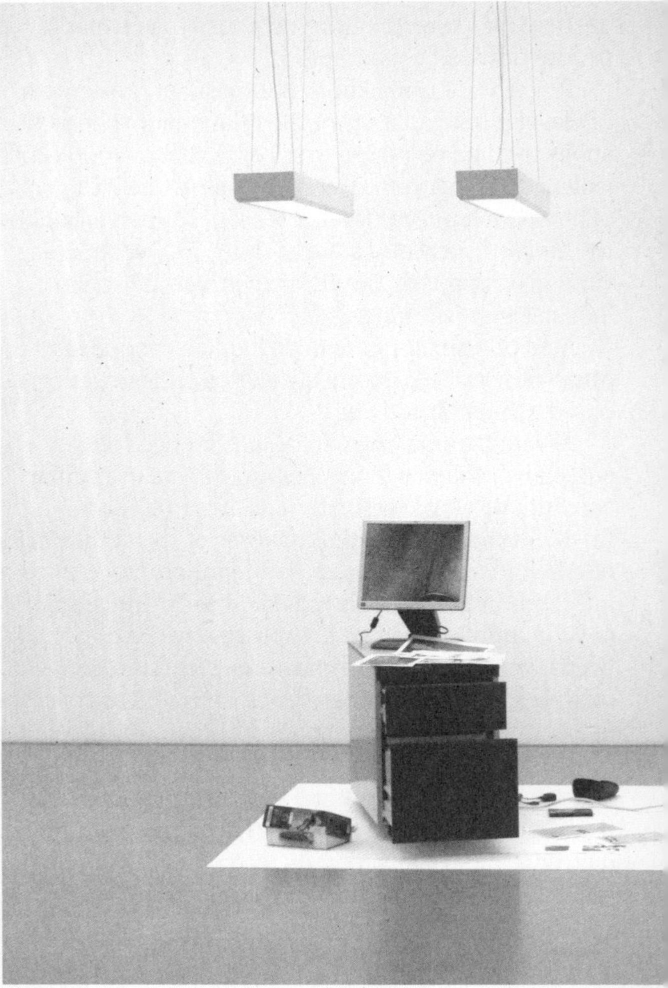

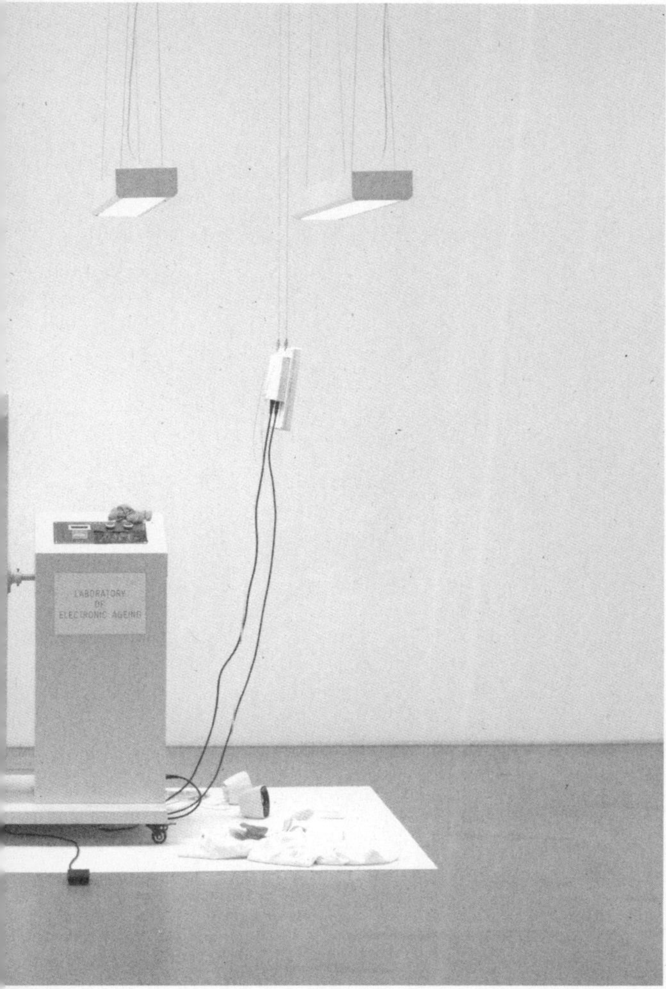

Dani Ploeger, *Laboratory of Electronic Ageing*, 2019. An industrial drop testing machine is exhibited in a museum. Instead of its intended use as a testing device in production and innovation processes it is put on display to endlessly drop an unused high-tech shaving device. While the shaver decomposes to a state of bare materiality, the industrial machine is symbolically disconnected from the realm of production and reintroduced as a creative instrument. © Dani Ploeger

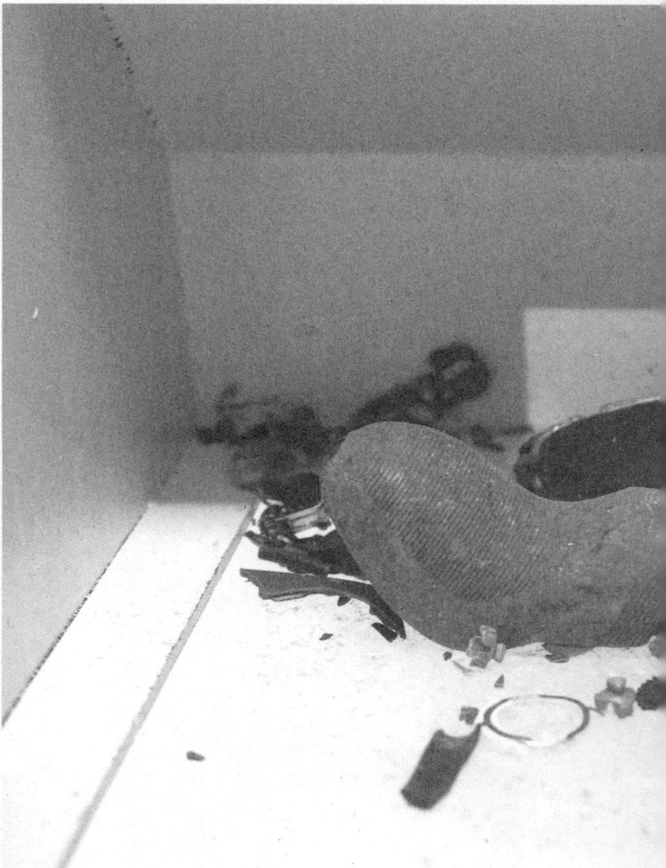

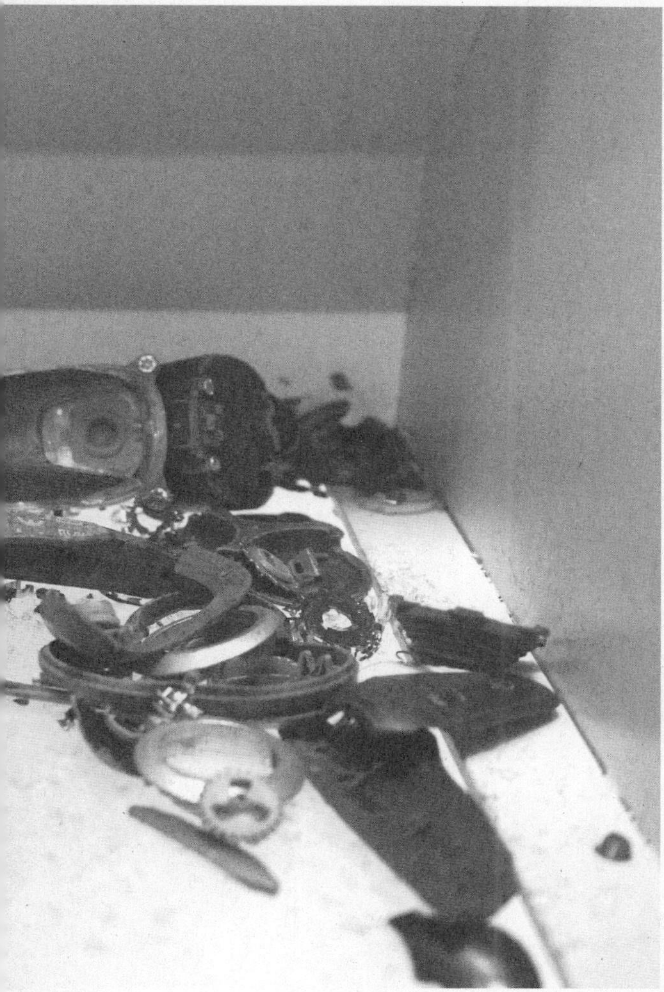

Dani Ploeger, *Laboratory of Electronic Ageing*, 2019.

matter

distribution

logistics⇝ part I

Elaine W. Ho & Florian Cramer

Elaine W. Ho & Florian Cramer

The following edited correspondence ran in parallel to shipment HQL-364 from Rotterdam to Hong Kong through the network of LIGHT LOGISTICS, a project initiated and coordinated by the 'now and again exhibition space, *distribution* service, thematic inquiry, and sometimes shop in Kowloon, Hong Kong', Display Distribute. LIGHT LOGISTICS is a 'person-to-person distribution network enabled by the surplus carrying power of couriers' and 'a free but not-in-time service'.

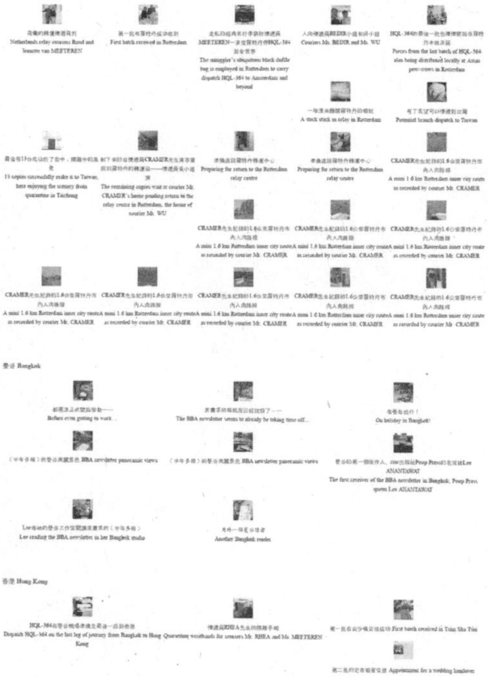

The LIGHT LOGISTICS log references the hard tracking of global courier systems, yet with the wobbling reliability of gossip and uneven distribution of timing and information as its highlight terms of service. There is a clarity of transaction in that publications from our distro may be purchased, and points A and B are designated by where the book begins (most often from our relay centre in Hong Kong, but sometimes also directly from the publisher) and where the reader-receiver is located. But in and around that there is a narrative arc that makes space for all kinds of action and relation to occur, if one pays enough attention.
Couriering becomes a physical linkage imbued with other potentiality, because the courier is very often a reader or bookmaker herself, or becomes one. In this sense, our enterprise feels more akin to the challenge of Ursula K. Le Guin's 'Carrier Bag Theory of Fiction'—a strange realism composed of the banal details of moving things from one place to another, begging other possibilities for the ways we inscribe the world.[1]

1. 'Getting a Move On: A Logistics of Thought towards Print and Publics', Elaine W. Ho.

2020-11-04

Hello Elaine,
Are you familiar with mail artist Ulises Carrión's projected courier system E.A.M.I.S. ('Erratic Art Mail International System') from 1977? It was preceded by an essay 'Mail Art and the Big Monster' in which he wrote:

> Mail art uses as support the postal system—a complex, international system of transport, including thousands of people, buildings, machinery, world treaties, and God knows what. The proof that the post is not the medium is that to use it, an artist dœsn't need to understand how it functions. Even in the utopic possibility that the artist reaches complete understanding of the system, he cannot control it.
> ... All I know is that there is a Monster, and that by posting all sorts of mail pieces, I am knocking at his door.

To quote from the EAMIS manifesto:

> An alternative to the official Post Offices.
>
> 1.
>
> The E.A.M.I.S will carry messages in any format: cards, letters, parcels, etc, and realized in any medium—book, cassette, tape, film, etc.
>
> 2.
>
> The message must reach the E.A.M.I.S office by any way other than the official Post Offices. It can be delivered by the author or by any other person. ...
>
> 8.
>
> By using the E.A.M.I.S you support the only alternative to the national bureaucracies and you strengthen the international artists community.

Ulises Carrión (Post Master)

Florian

2020-11-14

Dear Florian,
Yes, I found it poignant that at the beginning of the Covid-19 pandemic in the West there was a sudden interest in one-on-one correspondences again—even e-mail chain letters started to resurface in my inbox. Of course, with the diminishing of face-to-face contact the opening of other channels by which intimacy and affect can travel makes perfect sense. The LIGHT LOGISTICS project of Display Distribute is viewed in mainland China and Hong Kong much more through this social lens than as the larger inquiry into infrastructure that we discuss ourselves. At least from my own point of view as a courier, these are the kinds of comments we hear most from receivers and other participating couriers, because the real-life interactions logisticking garners are completely different encounters than would happen otherwise with the commercial courier companies that everyone has now grown accustomed to in their daily lives. We find out we have friends in common, we tell one another our travel plans, there are publishing projects and even the sharing of pet photos among strangers. Maybe it's a bit mundane or trite, but the also banal question of slowness that is intertwined with these interactions and journeys is one of the most important aspects of reconsidering how globalization, technology, and infrastructure affect our relations to the world and with one another.
Best,
e

2020-11-11

Dear Elaine,
My friend Goodiepal (musician, one-of-a-kind-person, and community activist living in Copenhagen) runs a similar courier system where people send postal mail to his mother or grandmother [*he doesn't have an e-mail address*]/Friends pick it up and physically deliver it to him wherever in the world he is. His collective (Goodiepal & Pals) now also runs a courier/smuggling operation to bring refugees over the EU border in Serbia.
-F

2020-11-10

Dear Florian,
Goodiepal, yes! It sounds like his European underground railroad is a heroic form of subterfuge from which we could learn more and exchange with. It has also always been our main reference to think through smugglers and pirates and parallel traders. With the fragile relations between Hong Kong and the mainland being the very first impetus, the transition toward focusing upon publications being carried across borders has very much to do with the sensitivity of content and those risks involved. As an aside, I like very much the use of the word 'sensitivity' when discussing the sociopolitical 'appropriateness' of content in the Chinese context. Other countries get a good laugh about China announcing more than often enough about its 'feelings' being hurt by other countries, but what is acute about this notion is that it does not remove the realm of aesthetics and the affective from politics as most nation states pretend to do in the name of a general welfare. Regardless, for us to slip the most personal and/or minute of encounters into a structure that does not need them could perhaps be described as a soft call to sensitize, weaken, or slow down the slick and steely frames that infrastructure and contemporary logistics⤳ advance.

Today I had an interesting conversation with members of the Laboratory of Insurrectionary Imagination and a few others, and JJ recalled how when they were doing interventions in the finance district of New York—I think in the early 2000s—wanting to learn all about finance as a means towards dismantling capitalism. But later, they grew to think that you don't need to understand the system if you really want to smash it, because dismantling goes beyond reform;

the real goal would be to build up something completely other...

I don't necessarily agree with this thought, though the degree of how much one should understand what one wants to infiltrate, rework, dismantle, and so on, needs to be addressed. It is notable, nevertheless, that Carrión also premises the ignorance of the artist as part of his manifest.

There was a period in my logistics⇝ fervour where I wanted to take online courses in industrial logistics⇝ in order to understand the frameworks better, but perhaps intuitively the scale didn't reach me down here in the shadowy realm of one-to-one exchanges... I have, however, investigatively engaged in some cross-border parallel trading of luxury cosmetics and milk powder! Greetings from Guangzhou,
e

↣

2020-11-18

While reading your text 'Getting a Move On: A Logistics of Thought towards Print and Publics', I was reminded of a discussion on piracy with Raqs Media Collective circa fifteen years ago that taught me about my (and generally Western) biases in perspectives on piracy. Back then, piracy was largely discussed in the context of download culture (with The Pirate Bay, Library.nu/LibGen, aaaaarg & WaReZ servers as the standard examples), but Raqs brought in the perspective of pirated software and DVDs sold on street markets. (I wonder whether that culture and economy still exist. When I moved to my neighbourhood in Rotterdam, it was still normal that when you went to a hairdresser, mobile vendors of pirated DVDs would come by and sell you the latest Hollywood films.) Back then, I largely shared the view of the Free Software/Open Source movement that intellectual property should end but that the piracy of commercial software ultimately had the effect of keeping the software industry in business↦— preventing a mainstream success of Free Software. Raqs, however, argued in favour of considering pirate work as a form of community care addressing real community needs, which then made me rethink my position. Nevertheless, I'm still torn on this issue. If one just sticks to the example of digital piracy, then one could argue that The Pirate Bay paved the way for Netflix, LibGen paved the way for Amazon Kindle, and WaReZ servers paved the way for App Stores; not only conceptually or in their user interface design, but also in the 'content' they provided. (The Pirate Bay offered pretty much the same kind of mainstream films that are offered by Netflix, and so on).
-F

E: There is a great text from Lawrence Liang (also a frequent collaborator with Raqs), Prashant Iyengar and Jiti Nichani called '*How Does an Asian Commons Mean*', and it offers exactly a varying genealogy from which to historically and culturally understand piracy and versioning as a process of commoning. It was written some years ago and maybe also does not resolve the quandary you mention regarding how digital piracy and FLOSS (Free Libre and Open Source Software) movements have provided fodder for the strengthened barricades of corporate platforms⇛, but this cat-and-mouse game was always the case, wasn't it?
F: In my view, Open Source and piracy activists are still far ahead of contemporary art institutions in their rejection of property and alternative visions of ownership and public distribution. But I also tend to find those debates in FLOSS, piracy and associated art practices being stuck in discourses of the 1990s. They tend to get deadlocked in technicalities of media, and in debates on how to keep channels open. Therefore, I am very much in tune with Display Distribute and how it has shifted all these questions to: 'who will transport it?' and 'who will read it?'

(correspondence continued in collective organization⇛)

↣

feeding

Thalia Hoffman

To eat is a basic need for living. However, it is much more than merely a physical need. *Feeding* and eating have always been part of socio-political, economic, and cultural frames of thinking and of decision-making. The priorities of these frames, or belief systems, decide upon our eating habits, such as religious food traditions and regulations, the distribution↣ of nutrition supplies around the globe or determine certain foods as expensive or cheap. Feeding and eating also play a major role in the construction of subjective identities. Personal selections of certain ingredients, specific cooking methods and ceremonial eating habits tend to characterize human beings, individually as well as socially. Therefore, feeding and eating are not only things one does to maintain one's body, but a fundamental part of many aspects of life.

Feeding and eating is something one can do for oneself, but it is not an action that is possible without co-relations and interactions with others (animals, plants, the land, and so on). Today, after almost two years of a global pandemic, social distancing has forced people to stay apart and encouraged them not to exchange physical particles. I propose that feeding as a performative tactic of critical making↬ might teach us something about how to nourish each other again.

In my artistic practice I use feeding and eating as performative research. I construct participatory meals as a critical reflection on and digestion of processes of socio-political constructions and individual choices. tactics[1] are time-based opportunities that we can seize to change or influence the mechanism we are a part of. As such, tactics do not overturn the ruling system, but use opportunities to strike at specific junctures.[2]

1. I use the term tactic following Michel de Certeau's use of the term in practices of everyday life.
2. Michel de Certeau, Fredric Jameson and Carl R. Lovitt, 'On the Oppositional Practices of Everyday Life', *Social Text* 3 (Autumn 1980), pp. 3–43.

Through the ongoing series of performances entitled *To Serve You*, I propose a critical performative tactic that explores the power relations between feeder and eater. It is an intimate performance series which explores elements of feeding and the power relations established in feeding through passion, pleasure, and compassion alongside organization, supervision, and imposing.

To Serve You practices and examines feeding and the interrelationship it creates between feeders, eaters, and food. The performances engage all five senses—seeing, hearing, tasting, smelling, and touching—and the digestion and olfactory systems of the participants. Feeding as a performative tactic activates participants and viewers directly and physically, through the body. *To Serve You* addresses exterior as well as interior parts of the body, penetrating one's physical experience in an attempt to raise a socio-political resistance from within. Philosopher Maurice Merleau-Ponty argues that 'The perceiving subject is not this absolute thinker; rather, it functions according to a natal pact between our body and the world, between ourselves and our body.'[3] The performance series *To Serve You* enters every gateway into one's body to activate socio-political critical thinking.

Feeding as a performative tactic arouses direct and intimate inter-relations between feeder and eater, and between the members of a group of eaters. In agreeing to eat something, the eater accepts something foreign to become part of his/her body. 'The classification of something as food means it is understood as

3. Maurice Merleau-Ponty, 'An Unpublished Text by Maurice Merleau-Ponty: A Prospectus of His Work', in *The Primacy of Perception and Other Essays on Phenomenological Psychology, the Philosophy of Art, History, and Politics*, ed. J.M. Edie, trans. A.B. Dallery (Evanston, IL: Northwestern University Press, 1964), p. 5.

something made to become part of who we are.'[4] According to philosopher Deane Curtin, humans have a physical understanding that anything they eat will become part of their bodily self. As such, according to Curtin, food holds a special relation to the Self. In the performance series *To Serve You* I, as the main feeder, draw attention to this physical understanding, while participants are challenged to respond and to interact with what might be transferred into their body and become part of them.

Feeding inherently contains power relations between the one who feeds and the one who eats. The power relations can be found within personal relationships, as well as between humans and institutions-⊕›, and people amid their socio-political community. Surprisingly these power relations are neither clear nor stable and tend to change throughout various feeding interactions. *To Serve You* seeks to explore the connection between food, rules, law, nationality, and security through the power relations between guest/host, feeder/eater and among the diners.

In a century in which everyday life is flooded with images, moving images and sounds, I choose to infiltrate all of the bodily senses, so that my practice can be experienced through the body as well as inside the body. To me this is especially urgent, since the local socio-political conflicts of the area east to the Mediterranean, where I live, are vigorously interpreted, visually and vocally. Between news, TV-shows, films, blogs, and academic research in various fields, endless information has been and is being communicated, documented, and recorded regarding the conflicts in this area. I experiment with senses and inner parts in

4. Deane W. Curtin, 'Food/Body/Person', in *Cooking, Eating, Thinking: Transformative Philosophies of Food*, ed. Deane W. Curtin and Lisa M. Heldke (Bloomington: Indiana University Press, 1992), pp. 3–22, p. 9.

order to explore the possibilities of embodying socio-political critical thinking and making↬. These experiences are a result of both dissatisfaction with communicating only through sight and sound, and of my eagerness to subversively interact and affect participants through my practice.

to serve you—a performance series (2017–ongoing)

The first realization of the performance series was part of the exhibition 'Motions for the Agenda' (curated by Avi Feldman in collaboration with Vardit Gross, Artport 2017). First as a series of dinners with jurists, culture scholars, sociologists, and psychologists in which we talked about feeding while being fed by me, held at The Israeli Center for Digital Art in Holon. These dinners were recorded, then edited and mixed into a sound work. The next step, inspired by the sound work, was an intimate dinner performance of a seven-course vegetarian meal performed by three feeders to an audience of six eaters.

Since then, *To Serve You* performs in different venues, it continuously adjusts itself to the changing socio-political and environmental surroundings alongside the performance location and the number of eaters and feeders.

Performers: Michal Samama, Carmel Bar, Ofri Omer, Shailoh Phillips, Thalia Hoffman.

↣

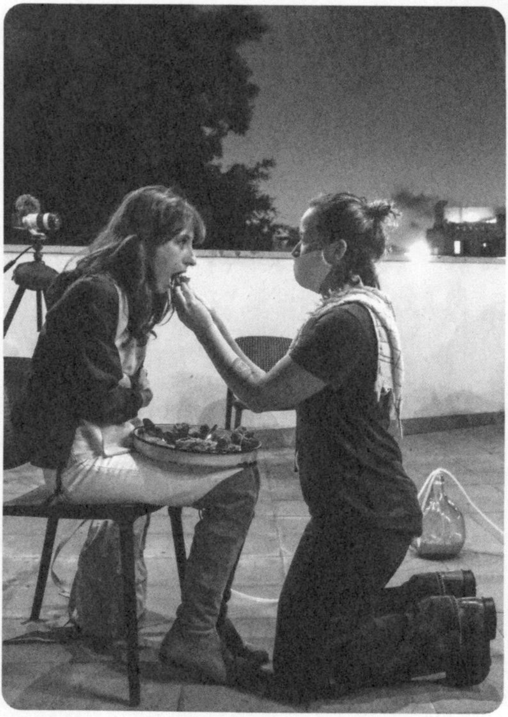

To Serve You, HaBait Theatre, Tel Aviv, 2020, photos: Uri Rubinstein. ▲ ▶

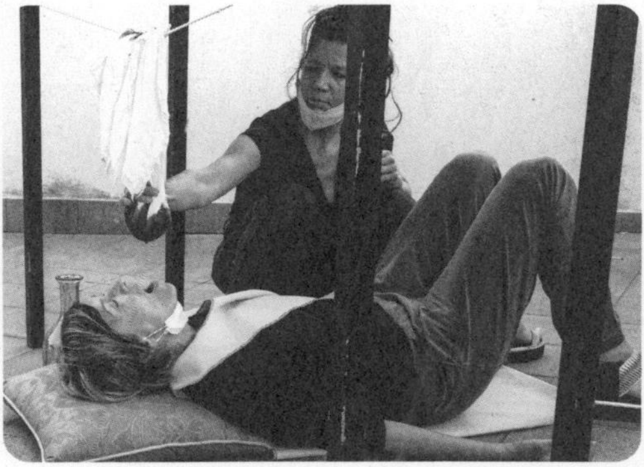

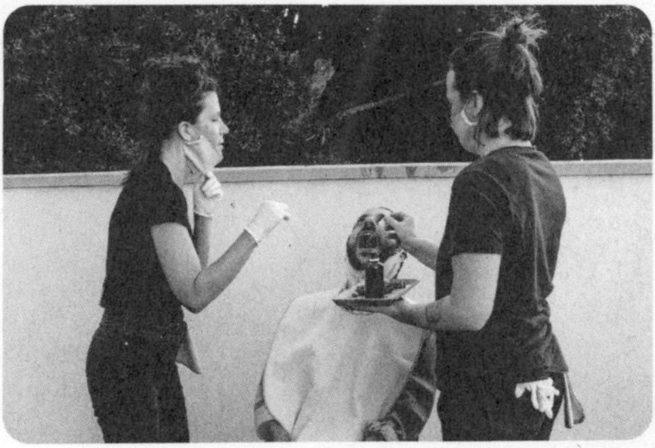

grammatography

Akiem Helmling

↣

Writing is a material practice↣, consisting of two associated activities: the creation and composition of signs. This makes it a fundamentally collective material practice↣. Additionally, all writing can be reproduced, transported, adapted, rewritten, repurposed, reshaped, and shared with comparatively little effort and cost. Therefore, writing arguably is one of the most collective material practices↣ in existence.

With the introduction of variable fonts by Adobe, Apple, Google, and Microsoft in September 2016, the stage was set for grammatographic writing, whereby letters are dynamic instead of static. In variable fonts, letter outlines no longer have a static contour, but can be modified by the writer into different shapes according to parameters predefined by the designer. For example, a letter no longer needs to be written in predefined weights such as normal or bold type (as is the case with static fonts), but can now be written in any of the intermediary shapes between normal and bold. Also, dynamic fonts or 'grammata' can provide more advanced capabilities whereby letters can be transformed into completely different shapes, defined by the person writing with them. Currently, we can understand this innovation and its potential for transforming cultures of writing only through old concepts and conventions—namely traditional, static-outline fonts and typography. In order to grasp its future potential, we propose a new term: *grammatography*↣: writing with prefabricated dynamic letters. These can change their shape during and even after the act of writing.

The term grammatography explicitly contrasts this new method of writing with the ones we are currently using: chirography and typography. When writing by hand, also known as chirography, writers generate the letters themselves while writing text, in contrast to

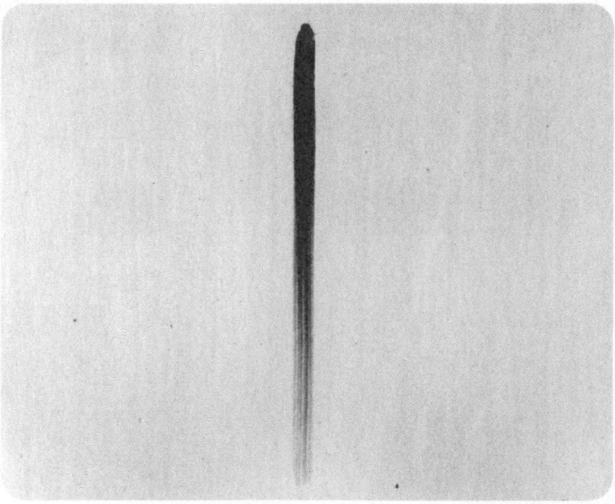

Lee Ufan, *From Line*, 1978, glue, stone pigment on canvas, 182 x 227 cm, www.studioleeufan.org.

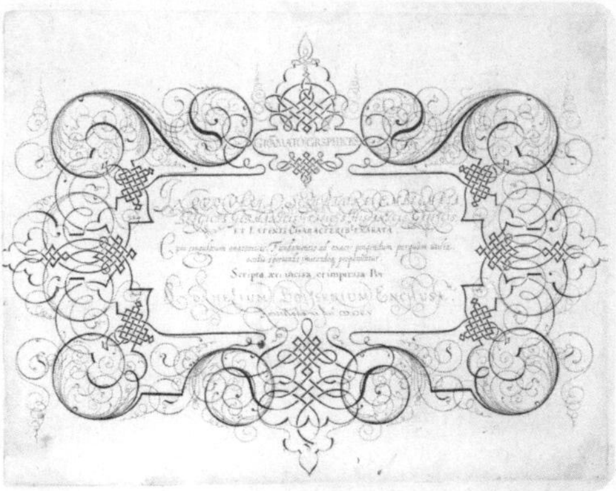

Grammato-Graphices, in: *Quo Varia Scripturae Emblemata*, Cornelis Dirckszoon Boissens (1568–1634), 1605, Rijksmuseum, Amsterdam.

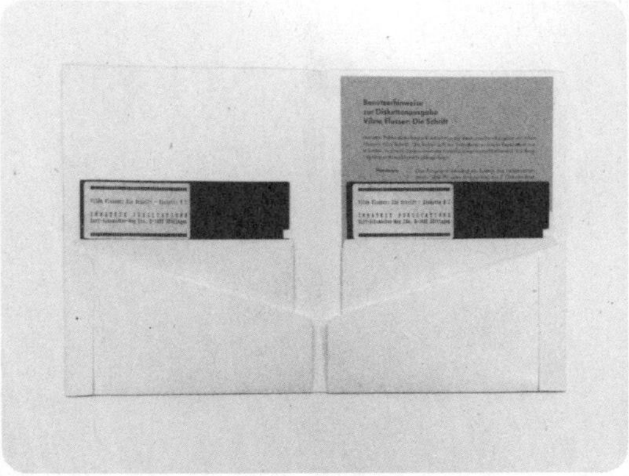

Vilém Flusser, *Die Schrift* – Floppy Disk Edition (European Photography), 1987, www.flusser-archive.org.

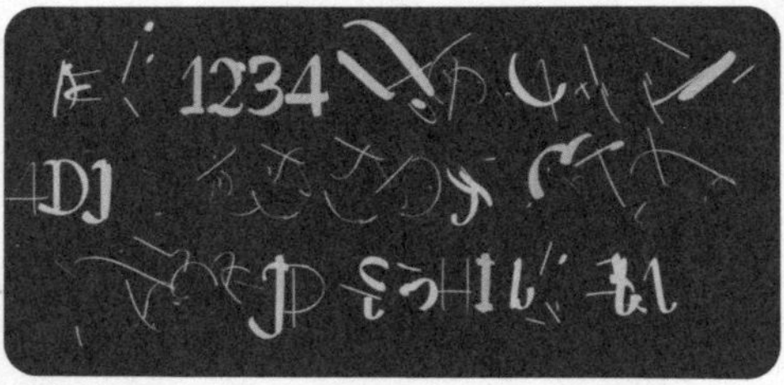

Underware, Penstrument, A Grammatographic Synthesizer, 2020, Underware.nl.

typography where writers use pre-fabricated letters (nearly always designed by another person) to compose their own words, sentences, and texts. Typography enables distribution↣ of texts in large editions, whereby each copy is 100% identical and whose letters remain the same forever (if one leaves aside the material wear of ink and paper). 500 years after the famous Gutenberg Bible (also known as the 42-line Bible or just B42) was printed, this is still the most common way of sharing information and communicating in writing.

While Gutenberg was definitely not the first person to use prefabricated letters, he was arguably most influential for the chirographic to typographic transformation of the Western world. Many have written and published about the societal impact of the Gutenberg press, for example Marshall McLuhan, Neil Postman, Vilém Flusser, and Eric A. Havelock. While Flusser is known for his claim that (human) history only started with the act of writing, it is perhaps even more important to recognize to which extent human life is informed by how we write. Up to now, Western modernity has been clearly a typographic one, if only due to the fact that all laws are published in static typographic writing.

But with the introduction of variable fonts, grammatography has become widely available and promises to disrupt this foundational technology undergirding modernity.

There is a clear connection between grammatography and the internet, or more precisely, the technologies that constitute the World Wide Web: the hypertext transfer protocol (http) in conjunction with the hypertext markup language (html) and its ↣ extensions CSS and Javascript. This combination of network protocol, file format and, optionally, computer programming language augment linear text into hypertext. However, this technology still only makes the structure of a text dynamic, not the shape of its letters.

In the early days of the internet, most people only understood hypertext as a variation of the static text, and therefore borrowed typographic terminology such as headers, footers, and pages from the foregoing typographic age. Vilém Flusser, however, immediately understood the novelty and consequence of this new technology. When he published a hypertext version of his book *Die Schrift* in 1987, he wisely and presciently called this publication neither an e-book nor an electronic publication, but simply a 'nicht mehr Buch' ('no longer book').

Along the same lines, we could ask whether a letter whose shape can be dynamically changed is still a letter, or whether it is rather a no-longer-letter. Can writing with dynamic letters even be compared with the writing of static letters, or writing by hand?

Grammatography has to do with letters, to the degree that both the writer of the text and the designer of the letters are involved in defining the letter shapes. As such, grammatography could be understood as a new form of writing in addition to our existing forms of writing, an act in which we use new sorts-of-writing instruments, in the same way as we play different musical instruments. The result is an interplay of the performer and instrument builders. Both instruments are characterized by flexible, built-in general vocabularies that are subsequently performed; in music, musical scales like the chromatic scale, in text, script likes Latin script.

Grammatography can open up as many possibilities for writing as musical instruments can for making sound. While we primarily play musical instruments for aesthetic reasons (expressions of feelings instead of communicating precise messages), a similar expressive range could (re)emerge in this new kind of writing. Grammatography points to a form of writing that transcends the currently dominant typographic logic of writing, and frees the act of writing from its typographic imprisonment.

A historical note: the term grammatography was first used in 1605, in a publication in which the Dutch calligrapher Cornelis Dirckszoon Boissens demonstrated his penmanship. Its full title is *Grammato-Graphices. In Quo Varia Scripturae Emblemata* ('Grammato-Graphices. Containing Various Illustrations of Handwriting'). In 1861, grammatography was also used in the English translation of the German publication *Alphabete orientalischer und occidentalischer Sprachen: Grammatography: a Manual of Reference to the Alphabets of Ancient and Modern Languages*. Why the translator chose this term is unknown. Finally, the word grammatography appears in *De la grammatologie* (1967) by Jacques Derrida. Here, the term is used as a synonym for calligraphy. Finally in 2019, the Dutch type foundry Underware proposed to use this term for every kind of writing that involves dynamic letters. This proposal was made in response to the technical invention of variable fonts.

↣

grounded

Femke Snelting

↣

Yet another online meeting, in the fall of 2020. A festival will take place on the cusp of water and land, and the artists are preparing site-specific installations. As they present their projects to each other, one of them claims to be based in the particular area and persistently invites the artists calling in from remote locations to 'come over for a boat trip, and stick their boots in the mud'. There is no doubt that the best way to get to grips with the shifting grounds of the festival location will be to step on site.

Physical presence, and direct contact with the specific muddiness of a terrain can be part of a situated knowledge practice, a powerful antidote to presumed positions of exteriority and views from nowhere. But it is also a proprietary *gesture*⇢ that essentializes territorial nearness. It counts on the privilege of individual experience, and relies on touch at first hand or boot, sticking to knowledge that can only be acquired by presence. Centring on what can be perceived from where one is standing is taking a risk to foreground what is here and now, and to negate interdependencies that operate at a distance. How long did it take for the sediment to be deposited? Where will the polluted soil from the estuary eventually end up? When did the seagrass become invasive, or start capturing carbon?

In their work on touch, feminist thinker Karen Barad propose that 'being in touch' is what allows experiments to become participative, rather than remaining at some remove. They invite us to explore queer ways of being in touch, which involve (other-than-human) others besides ourselves:

> Thinking has never been a disembodied or uniquely human activity. Stepping into the void, opening to possibilities, straying,

going out of bounds, off the beaten path—diverging and touching down again, swerving and returning, not as consecutive moves but as experiments in in/determinacy.[1]

The kind of touch Barad propose is not counting on the legibility of what it steps into, nor on the reassuring effects of affection. As they remind us elsewhere, for a physicist, touch is but a sensation caused by electromagnetic repulsion.[2]

How to be *grounded*, without getting stuck in the mud of personal experience? I guess I am trying to re-articulate 'grounded' as a 'thinking-and-making-with' that is always already part of what it steps into. A grounded practice that does not depend on knowing where the ground begins or ends, and can let go of pre-established notions of fore-ground and back-ground.

Ground and feet, land and movement, verticality and time, situatedness and axes: the more of them we take into account when giving account of the spheres we share, the more degrees of freedom we are going to endow

1. Karen Barad, 'On Touching: The Inhuman That Therefore I Am', *differences* 23, no. 3 (2012), pp. 206–23.
2. Karen Barad, 'TransMaterialities: Trans*/Matter/Realities and Queer Political Imaginings', *GLQ: A Journal of Lesbian and Gay Studies* 21, nos. 2–3 (2015), pp. 387–422.

our deterritorialized and reterritorialized lives with.[3]

To be grounded means to be porous to remote impressions, to trust the touching done by (other-than-human) others, and to take into account that which it is caught up with, especially when it is not understood, can not be felt or ever be intuited. Because however distant, our deterritorialized and reterritorialized experiences are simply always in touch.[4]

3. Possible Bodies, 'No Ground', *Volumetric Regimes: Material Cultures of Quantified Presence* (Open Humanities Press, in press).
4. Kathryn Yusoff, 'Insensible Worlds: Postrelational Ethics, Indeterminacy and the (k)Nots of Relating', *Environment and Planning D: Society and Space* 31, no. 2 (2013), pp. 208–26.

material practice

Janneke Wesseling

Over the past decades, a re-evaluation or even rehabilitation of practice in relation to theory can be witnessed in the field of the humanities. New Materialist modes of thinking are largely accountable for this change in perspective on the role of practice in academic research. In the humanities, 'practice' has long been, and often still is, regarded as subordinate and subservient to theory. Many scholars look down on practice as being merely the handwork in the laboratory that is needed to support or provide proof of theory. The truly important work is of a theoretical nature, that is, the work of the mind. The hegemony of theory largely explains the struggle of art academies in Europe to gain recognition for artistic research↬ by universities (see artistic research↬).

From a historical point of view, the binary understanding of concept and matter, of subject and object, and the hierarchy of theory over practice in Western culture originated in the age-old tradition of valuing *vita contemplativa* over *vita activa*. The predominance of mind over body can be traced back to Plato and to Saint Augustine's embracing of platonic thinking, as argued by Hannah Arendt in *The Life of the Mind* (1978). Like Plato, Aristotle held deductive thinking in high esteem and downplayed experiment. Aristotle's *Categories* became formative of and canonical to medieval scholasticism.

According to American philosopher Ian Hacking (*Representing and Intervening*, 1983), the imbalance of theory and experiment was reversed with the scientific revolution of the seventeenth century, in particular with the thinking of Francis Bacon (1561–1626). During the scientific revolution, practical experiment 'was officially declared to be the royal road to knowledge, and the schoolmen were scorned because they argued from books instead of observing the world around them'.[1] But times have changed, Hacking tells us, and today the history of the sciences is almost always written as a history of theory rather than of experiment: philosophers of science 'constantly discuss theories and representations⊕› of reality, but say almost nothing about experiment, technology, or the use of knowledge to alter the world'. Hacking also notes that the theory/experiment status difference is 'modelled on social rank'. His *Representing and Intervening* contests the theory-dominated history of science. It is Hacking's conviction that 'a question posed in terms of theory and experiment is misleading because it treats theory as one rather uniform kind of thing and experiment as another'.[2]

For Hacking, practice is characterized by experiment and by the intervention in reality (instead of the representation⊕› of reality). Hacking calls himself an 'ontological realist' who believes the entities, states and processes described by correct theories are real, and not mere 'constructs of the human mind for organizing our experiments'.[3] In a certain respect, Hacking's *Representing and Intervening* anticipates New Materialist modes of thinking.[4] Under the heading of New Materialism, a diverse group of thinkers is brought together who, despite differences in outlook, agree in one fundamental respect: the existence of a reality, or of a world, of objects *out there*, independent of our gaze and of our knowledge of them, independent also of our access to these objects.

1. Ian Hacking, *Representing and Intervening Introductory Topics in the Philosophy of Natural Science* (Cambridge: Cambridge University Press, 1983), p. 149.
2. Ibid., p. 162.
3. Ibid., p. 2.
4. The New Materialist strain of thinking goes by a number of different names, among which New Materialism, Object Oriented Ontology, and Speculative Realism.

These thinkers aim 'to preserve the autonomy and irreducibility of substance'.[5]

New Materialism embodies the attempt to sidestep the subject-object divide created by René Descartes and Enlightenment philosophers such as Hume and Kant. New Materialists aim to overcome the Cartesian worldview, that is, the subject-object distinction.

A leading proponent of the New Materialist strain of thinking is the American philosopher and physicist Karen Barad—even though she does not like to use the term New Materialism, preferring 'agential realism' in its stead. Agential realism is the attempt 'to rethink fundamental concepts that support binary thinking including the notions of matter, discourse, causality, agency, power, identity, embodiment, objectivity, space, and time.'[6]

Barad emphasizes that

> agential realism does not merely offer a new framework through which to understand the roles of the human *and* the nonhuman, the material *and* the discursive, but inquires into the very *practices* through which they are differentiated.[7]

It is not the scope of this text to offer an interpretation of Barad's thinking. What is important here is that Barad does not refer to matter as a fixed substance, but rather as a process of 'iterative intra-

5. Levi R. Bryant, *The Democracy of Objects* (Ann Arbor: Open Humanities Press, 2011), p. 26.
6. Karen Barad, *Meeting the Universe Halfway: Quantum Physics and the Entanglement of Matter and Meaning* (Durham and London: Duke University Press, 2007), pp. 25, 26.
7. Ibid., p. 66.

activity'. 'Matter', in her view, 'refers to phenomena in their ongoing materialization'.[8]

Now, how might this New Materialist account relate to what is generally understood as *material practice* in the discourse among artists? It must be noted that in artistic discourse material practice is not used in opposition to 'conceptual practice'. Put otherwise, in artistic discourse, a practice that takes physical material or materiality as point of departure is not necessarily opposed to a practice that is guided by an abstract idea. For artists, material practice and 'conceptual practice' are multi-layered terms that do not exclude one another. More than that, from the 1960s onward, conceptual artists sought to connect or entangle matter and idea, image and language, thematizing this connection through their work.[9]

Conceptual art practices therefore may be, and often are, rooted in materiality and in material processes. This is the reason why many so-called Conceptual artists (such as Lawrence Weiner) refuse to be categorized as such. 'Conceptual' here refers not so much to the 'art work as idea' but to art practices in which the process of art making is regarded as equally important or relevant as the eventual outcome of this

8. Ibid., p. 151.
9. An early case in point are the *Industrial Poems*, or plastic 'Plaques', produced by Marcel Broodthaers, 1968–1972. Broodthaers said of these plaques that they were a kind of rebuses, of which 'the reading is impeded by the image-like quality of the text and vice versa. The stereotypical character of both text and image is defined by the technique of plastic. They are intended to be read on a double level—each one involved in a negative attitude which seems to me specific to the stance of the artist: not to place the message completely on one side alone, neither image nor text.' In: 'Dix mille francs de récompense' (1974), reprinted in *Industrial Poems Marcel Broodthaers: The Complete Catalogue of the Plaques, 1968–1972*, ed. Charlotte Friling and Dirk Snauwaert (Brussels: WIELS; Berlin: Hatje Cantz, 2021), p. 9.

process (Cf Weiner: 'the piece need not be built')[10]. There is no hierarchy here of 'materiality' and 'conceptuality', and no hierarchy of theory and experiment. In conceptual art (not only referring to American Conceptual Art form the 1960s and 1970s, but in the broader sense of the word), the role and importance of critical reflection in the making process, and of theory in the physical experiment, is acknowledged. One might even argue that nowadays, under the 'postconceptual condition' (Peter Osborne), the conceptual nature of art practice is recognized as a *sine qua non.* Art practice is of a material as well as a conceptual nature at the same time. One might conclude that the traditional philosophical opposition of matter and concept, of practice and theory, is overcome or nullified here.

Examples in this book of the reciprocal entanglement of concept and matter are Femke Snelting's project at the Bidston Observatory in Liverpool (see Snelting on embeddednes⇢); Thalia Hoffman's performance *To Serve You* (in feeding⤔); or Kate Rich on business↦ (this book contains many more examples).

10. From Weiner's 'Statements': 1) The artist may construct the piece 2) The piece may be fabricated 3) The piece need not be built. The Statements were published in 1968 by Seth Siegelaub as artist book.

tanah

Bunga Siagian & Ismal Muntaha
(Jatiwangi art Factory)

↣

Tanah in Indonesian may be loosely translated to English as earth, soil, land, ground.

For the people of (the Indonesian district) Jatiwangi, *tanah* has been the essential element in their lives for over a hundred years. Along with agriculture, the production of roof tiles and bricks had been the main economic activity in the region, up until the early 2000s. When Jatiwangi art Factory (JaF) was founded in 2005, the roof tile industry was declining. The declining number of traditional brick factories was occurring alongside state development projects to advance Jatiwangi as a large manufacturing region, in response to larger free market demands. Slowly but surely, the *tanah* of Jatiwangi that was characteristic of the ingenious hands of the people—a solid identity of Jatiwangi—shifted its role to a land of new concrete factories. Most of the agricultural land was changed from productive food cultivation into land for housing, shopping, and many other infrastructures that come with urban development and growth.

Arief Yudi, co-founder of JaF, often asks guests, colleagues, and friends, 'What do you think an ideal city should be like?' This question, a strange one for cosmopolites who have no attachment to a single domain or territory, quietly problematizes the question of what is 'ideal'. It is a pivotal question for those who were born, live, work, and will die in the same place, here in Jatiwangi. Issues revolving around dignity, identity, and a way of life in the space we occupy in the present and future is at stake. This is firmly intertwined with JaF's artistic practices and even its very existence.

There is no other choice for the people of Jatiwangi but to defend their *tanah*—their land, their earth, their soil, their ground—that has provided for life and its own ecosystem for decades. Many collective methods, work forms, performative acts, understandings, and artistic practices have made *tanah* their centre as well as their subject. In these processes, *tanah* is being shaped, positioned, redefined, redignified, and its status restored. By defending *tanah*, the people of Jatiwangi prevail as a collective subject that remains whole in the face of state development projects that neglect the voices of this community. Up to this day, JaF's practices and efforts are still expanding. One of them is Kota Terakota (Terracotta City), the result of *saling bantu* (mutual assistance) between various parties and policy makers.

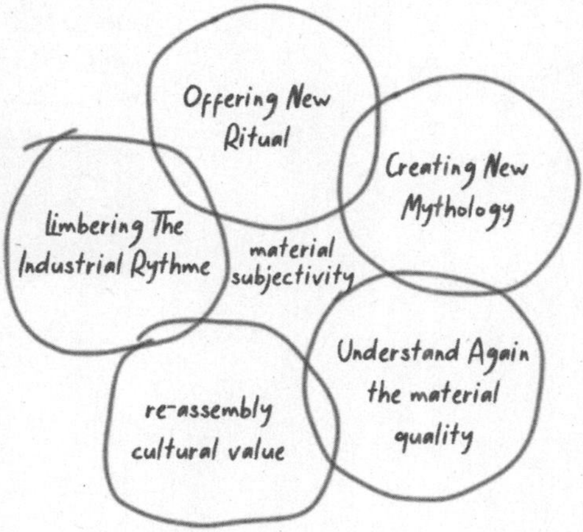

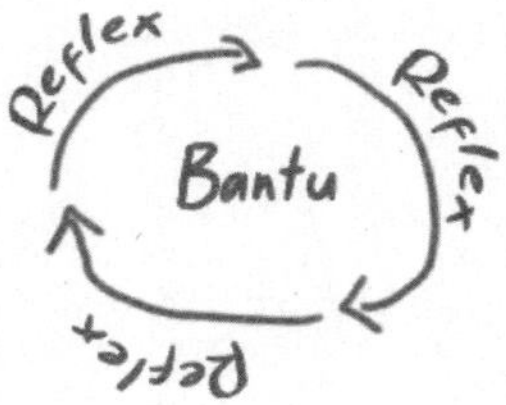
Reflex
Reflex
Bantu
Reflex

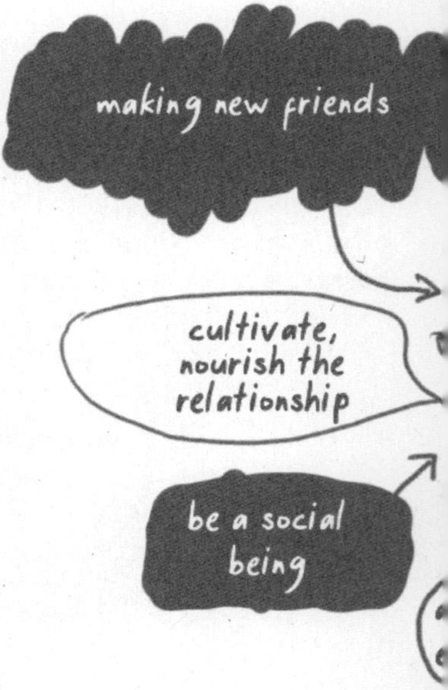
making new friends
cultivate,
nourish the
relationship
be a social
being

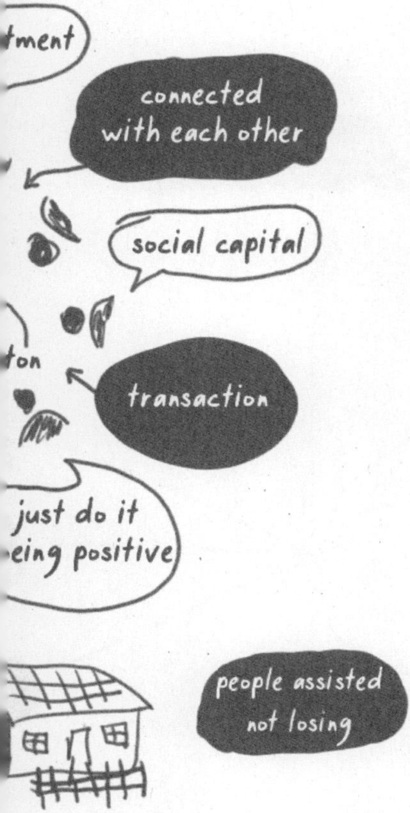
tment
connected with each other
social capital
ton
transaction
just do it
eing positive
people assisted not losing

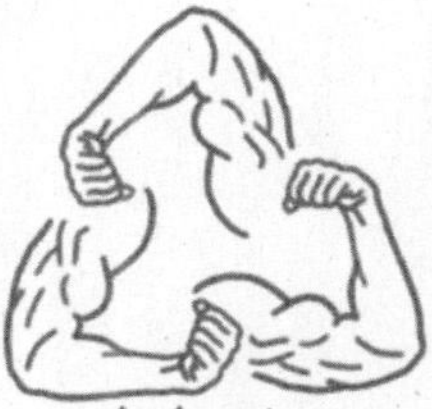

babanton

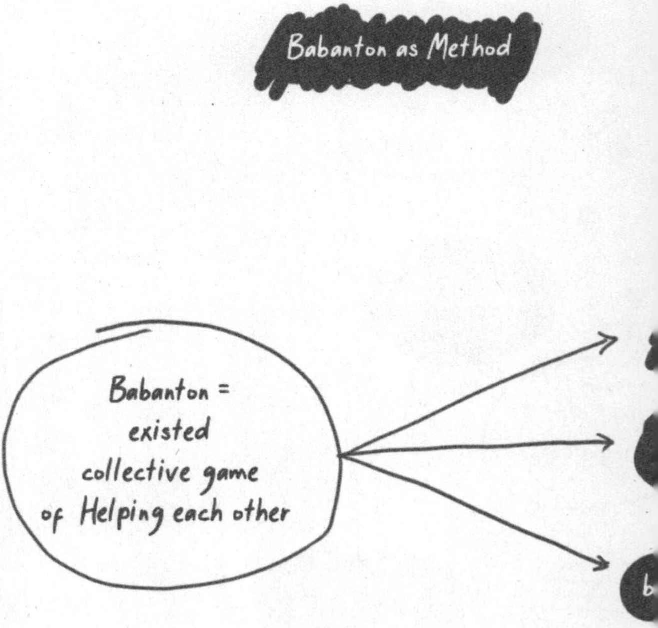
Babanton as Method
Babanton =
existed
collective game
of Helping each other

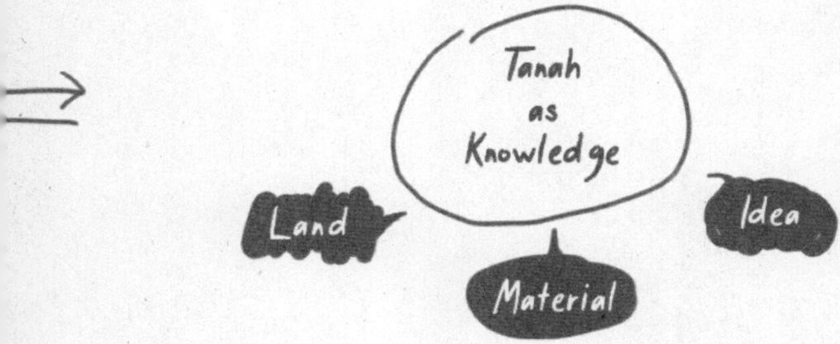
Tanah
as
Knowledge
Land
Material
Idea

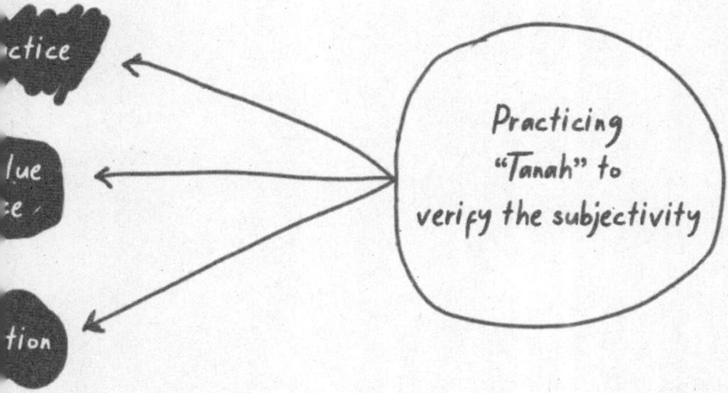
Practicing
“Tanah” to
verify the subjectivity

un
dis
cip
lin
ed

diy

Florian Cramer

Do-It-Yourself is a concept that has been (re-)invented multiple times throughout the twentieth and twenty-first centuries.

Originally, *diy* is a North American term for home improvement that has been in use since the 1950s.[1] Its close cousin is the French 'bricolage' both in its literal, everyday sense ('bricolage' hardware shops) and in its wider application in cultural anthropology and philosophy.[2] The literal meaning of diy is a material practice↣ of someone without professional training, typically in makeshift or even crude ways.

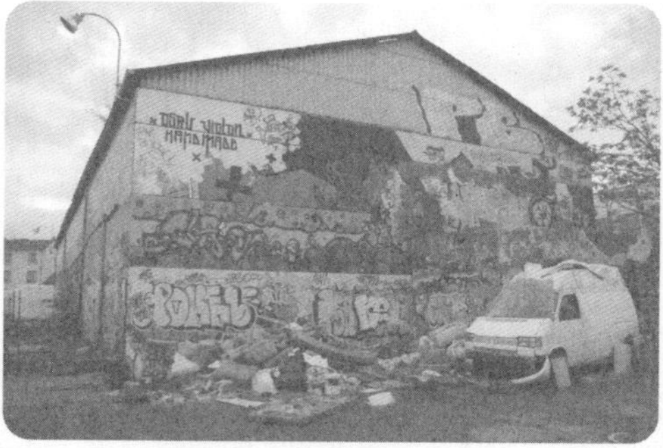

La Friche, former DIY space in Marseille, France, photo: Pascal Rey, 2008 (Creative Commons-BY-NC-SA 2.0).

Precursors to today's diy culture include the nineteenth-century Arts and Crafts movement and its self-built communities, Dadaism in Berlin in the 1920s with its slogan 'Dilettantes—rise up against art!', counter-culture experiments in the 1960s and 1970s

1. Garnet Hertz, 'Two Terms: Critical Making + D.I.Y.', *conceptlab.com*, 2020, conceptlab.com/2terms/pdf/hertz-2terms-202011181901.pdf.
2. Such as the concepts of philosophical 'bricolage' by Jacques Derrida and Claude Lévi-Strauss. Jacques Derrida, *Writing and Difference* (Chicago: University of Chicago Press, 1978 [1967]).

such as the *Survival Scrapbooks* of UK artist/musician/activist Stefan Szczelkun that taught readers how to build their own shelter, grow their own food and generate their own energy, and the media activism of the Raindance Corporation artist collective that published diy instruction manuals for building one's own radio and television broadcasting technology (critical making↝). These diy poetics were continued, among others, by the UK artists heath bunting and Kate Rich in the 1990s and in the contemporary zine series *Self-Reliance Library* of the Chicago-based Temporary Services collective.

Counter-cultural diy became commodified as early as in the 1970s with the *Whole Earth Catalog*,[3] an alternative lifestyle periodical and product catalogue. In the 1980s, the focus of its publishers shifted to home computing, early electronic social media and, ultimately, the Californian Internet economy.[4] Around the same time, punk and hip hop gave new meanings to diy. In punk, everyone could be their own fashion designer, a musician by playing only three guitar chords, and a graphic designer and publisher by making zines. Hip hop's early music production technology of scratching vinyl records was born out of poverty and diy improvisation.

These subcultures turned diy from merely a poetics (in the literal sense of poiesis as 'making↝') into a simultaneous poetics, aesthetics and—to some degrees —ethos and politics.

3. Diedrich Diederichsen and Anselm Franke, *The Whole Earth: California and the Disappearance of the Outside* (Berlin: Sternberg Press, 2013).
4. Fred Turner, *From Counterculture to Cyberculture: Stewart Brand, the Whole Earth Network, and the Rise of Digital Utopianism* (Chicago: University of Chicago Press, 2010).

⤳

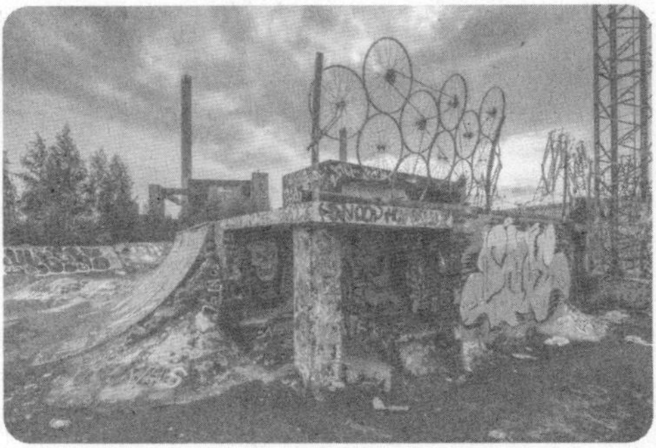

Suvilahti DIY skatepark in Kalasatama, Sörnäinen, Helsinki, Finland in June 2021, photo: Simo Räsäne (Creative Commons-BY-NC-SA 2.0).

diy since punk

In understandings of the term since the early 2000s, diy stands for an alternative to industrial capitalism and its products, and for the convergence of what used to be called 'alternative culture' and 'self-organized arts'.[5]

As opposed to the more established terms 'artist-run space' and 'artists collective/initiative', contemporary 'diy spaces' (that exist particularly in the USA) imply no clear-cut separation between artists and non-artists, professionals and non-professionals, and include artists of all trades, musicians, community organizers, political activists, squatters, bohemians, artists and their audiences. 'diy culture' in this sense has the connotation of cultural work that can no

5. Such as, comprehensively, in Amy Spencer, *DIY: The Rise of Lo-fi Culture* (New York: Marion Boyars, 2005).

longer be firmly placed under the moniker 'art', at least not fine art.[6]

Between the two extremes of diy as (a) counterculture and (b) home improvement stores there is the technological diy of hacker and 'maker' culture (critical making↚). With the boom of fab labs and maker spaces, this type of 'diy' has become its own industry.

Diy culture becomes problematic as a term if one extends the perspective to non-Western and non-industrialized countries where self-making and makeshift improvisation is not an exception, but the rule.

present

The Indonesian artist collective ruangrupa has been characterized as being driven by 'a strong diy ethos', born out of the necessity of creating one's own structures in post-dictatorship Indonesia and affinity and vicinity to 'punk and street cultures'.[7]

Subcultures and artist projects can converge in radical diy practices that are: self-taught, self-built, self-funded, happening in self-organized spaces using self-built infrastructure, with self-organized communication and distribution↣. 'Self' may refer to an individual, a collective or a community.

This makes diy a phenomenon that is concerned with autonomy. 'Autonomy', when translated literally from Greek to English, means 'self-governance'. In the

6. Although, historically, many contemporary art careers grew out of diy collectives. Examples include Gordon Matta-Clark and the FOOD restaurant collective of the early 1970s and Sherry Levine and Jenny Holzer as members of New York's Colab collective in the late 1970s to mid-1980s.
7. David Teh, 'Who Cares a Lot? Ruangrupa as Curatorship', *Afterall*, 2012, afterall.org/article /who-cares-a-lot-ruangrupa-as-curatorship.

context of artists' diy, autonomy is a poetics, and hence a categorically different notion of autonomy than that of aesthetic philosophy from Kant and Schiller to Adorno and Rancière. Instead of an idealist concept, autonomy becomes a material practice↣. Or perhaps more precisely: in diy culture, autonomy is being actively created—and permanently negotiated—in and through the material practice↣ of its community members. Re-applied to art, this means, to quote David Teh's characterization of ruangrupa, to further 'autonomy of artists, singular or plural, but not necessarily that of the artwork'.[8]

Building upon an Arts and Crafts legacy, diy culture is typically based on an explicit or implicit critique of disembodied and alienated industrial or institutional-⊕› production for which it creates hands-on alternatives. This critique and practice can have Marxist, left-anarchist, religious-spiritual, green-ecologist, conservative, liberal, libertarian, and extreme right-wing ideological underpinnings. Racist organic farmers, for example, neofascist squatters, Nazi rock bands, motorbike repair shops of outlaw biker clubs, religious cult communes and Alt-Right meme collectives are among those who practice and make up radical diy culture. This renders political-ethical claims for diy culture just as dubious as any other fundamental political-ethical claim for subculture, let alone any romanticization of minorities on the pure grounds of their minority position.

8. Ibid.

feral

Feral Atlas (Lili Carr & Feifei Zhou)

Feral⇝ is not necessarily a negative or positive word; it has different meanings in different contexts. In *Feral Atlas*, feral⇝ refers to a nonhuman entity (biological, chemical, geological) that is beyond human control.

feral⇝ effects are all around us. Flora and fauna adapt to and transform ecologies in tune with their own cycles and rhythms beyond the anticipation and control of human activities all the time. An apple tree thrives after a forest visitor tosses the core after eating an apple, for example.

The feral⇝ effects *Feral Atlas* is concerned with are the unexpected, non-designed consequences of human-made imperial and industrial infrastructures, which materially transform land, water, and air with such intensity that shifts occur in formally stable nonhuman ecologies. These shifts can create favourable conditions for living or non-living entities to run out-of-control, whose feral⇝ activities tip these ecologies from one state to another. Jellyfish caused ecological disaster in the Black Sea after being accidentally brought there in ballast water in cargo ships, for example.

feral⇝ effects occur across multiple, overlapping, and uneven scales and often go unnoticed and unattended—a consequence perhaps of the hubris of modernizing infrastructure projects—and so feral⇝ effects pile up. This accumulation of feral⇝ effects shifts interactions between humans and nonhumans across scales, creating new, life-threatening ecological conditions. This, *Feral Atlas* argues, is the more-than-human Anthropocene.

In these critical times we argue that we need urgently to learn methods and practices of attention to what our infrastructures do. Rather looking at feral⇝

effects as a result, *Feral Atlas* asks, what triggers and encourages them?[1]

workshop↦: feral atlas as a verb

You are invited to explore the more-than-human worlds of *Feral Atlas* > www.feralatlas.org.

Lili Carr & Feifei Zhou
Making Matters Symposium 2020, 20 November 2020 | Driving the Human Opening Festival, 22 November 2020

introduction: feral atlas as a verb

The *Feral Atlas* concept of **infrastructure-mediated state change** is where ongoing human-made infrastructural processes radically change environments to the point where our social and ecological systems are tipped from one state to another. In *Feral Atlas*, we call these infrastructural processes **Tippers**. Tippers are a non-exhaustive set of verbs that express the transformative actions of human-made infrastructures.

This workshop↦ is an experiment in noticing, recording, and expressing the actions of Tippers in our daily environments. Can we imagine ways of doing the infrastructural work we observe differently?[2]

1. During the symposium Making Matters: Collective Material Practices in Critical Times, we (*Feral Atlas* members Lili Carr and Feifei Zhou) conducted a group exercise in noticing feral⇝ effects in the area where you live. The workshop↦ instructions are reproduced below.
2. See Introduction to *Feral Atlas* and *Feral Atlas as a Verb: Beyond Hope and Terror* at www.feralatlas.org.

infrastructures

In *Feral Atlas*, infrastructures are technological apparatuses constructed to do kinds of work that (at least some) humans want done. *Feral Atlas* defines infrastructures in relation to three conditions:

1. Infrastructures are **material apparatuses** that affect landscapes, waterscapes, and airscapes.
2. Infrastructures are '**public works**' in the sense that they involve many people and projects, and are part of broadly imagined campaigns to change landscapes in the interests of some kind of governance programme.
3. Infrastructures are apparatuses created by **human design**.

See *Feral Atlas and the More-than-Human Anthropocene* at www.feralatlas.org.

tippers

To show how infrastructures create state changes, *Feral Atlas* starts with the kinds of work they are designed to do. We ask: In the process of doing that work, what gaps and rifts appear in the state of things? What disappears? What proliferates?

Feral Atlas expresses Tippers as eight one-syllable words, each derived from the early history of the English language, and, as such, at the base of English-speakers' experience. Consider these words as verbs; they describe things that people—and infrastructures—do. By classifying infrastructures according to these verbs, we aim to make clear the rifts that can appear when imperial and industrial modes of work take over from other ways of doing things.

— Notice **TAKE** as the action of 'taking'.
— Notice **SMOOTH/SPEED** as the action of 'smoothing/speeding'.
— Notice **PIPE** as the action of 'piping'.
— Notice **GRID** as the action of 'gridding'.
— Notice **CROWD** as the action of 'crowding'.
— Notice **BURN** as the action of 'burning'.
— Notice **DUMP** as the action of 'dumping'.

See *Tippers: Modes of Infrastructure-Mediated State Change* at www.feralatlas.org.

exercise

Take a walk outside in the area where you live. What infrastructural work do you observe in action? Which *Feral Atlas* Tipper(s) could describe this work?

Observe infrastructures working as they have been designed and built to do—not infrastructures that are being misused, or have broken down. Can you think of any other Tipper categories —other verbs—that could also describe this work?

Using video or sound recording, written text or spoken word, drawings, or photographs, try to capture directly the sounds and sights of infrastructural work and the scene in which this kind of infrastructural work is being done.

Feral Atlas uses short videos and sound pieces to convey something of the sheer power of Tippers, that is, their ability to rip apart existing social and ecological systems and to create new ones. This is just one of the ways Feral Atlas has attempted to capture the direct sounds, sights, and actions of infrastructural work. We encourage you to come up with others.

Please be prepared to share with the group your first-hand observations and recordings. Do you notice any feral⇝ entities that attune to the infrastructural work you observe?

Look together at the group's collection of observations and recordings. Notice the similarities in infrastructural actions manifest differently across scale, duration, and place. Can we imagine ways of doing the infrastructural work we observe differently?

For more *Feral Atlas* exercises, see *Feral Atlas Exercises*: Connecting the Material to the Place Where You Live *at www.feralatlas.org*.
The text for this brief has been adapted from *Feral Atlas: The More-Than-Human Anthropocene*. Curated and edited by Anna L. Tsing, Jennifer Deger, Alder Keleman Saxena and Feifei Zhou.

feral

Kate Rich

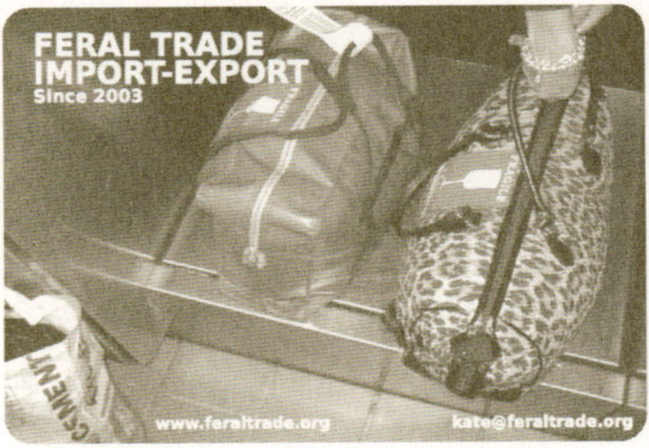
FERAL TRADE
IMPORT-EXPORT
Since 2003
www.feraltrade.org
kate@feraltrade.org

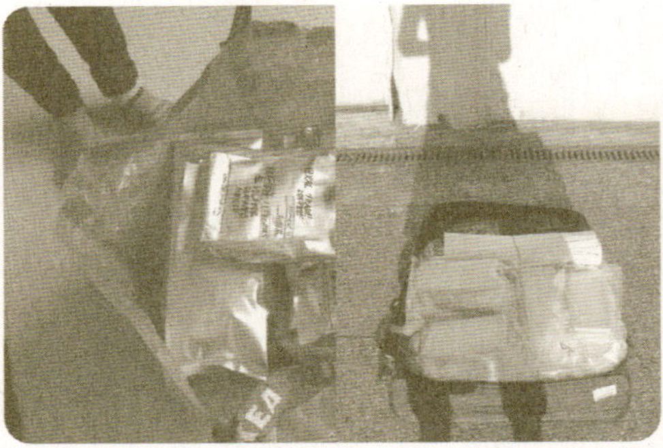

My interest in the *feral*⇝ comes from the vantage point of my own business↦ (see the entry for 'business↦' in this lexicon, with which this account is entwined). Feral Trade[1] is an artist-run grocery business↦ and underground freight network, trading coffee, olive oil, dried bamboo shoots and other vital goods outside official channels since 2003. All the suppliers and all of the customers come through extended social networks. Goods hitchhike in the spare baggage space of friends, colleagues and passing acquaintances, while museums, offices, hotel reception desks, and other quasi-public places act as trans-shipment points and depots. An operation effectively like DHL, but without any employees, vans, facilities, or attempted delivery notes and without a business↦ plan. While money does change hands, this is almost peripheral to the commitments and relations that keep the trade in motion. Instead, the core business↦ of Feral Trade is in forging vivid, resurgent, and sociable supply chains, outside the logic of the market.

Calling this operation feral⇝ was initially a knee-jerk reaction to the excessive truth claims that 'fair' and 'free' trade put out. I took up the word feral⇝ as an act of triangulation, connecting 'fair' and 'free' to feral⇝ to complicate or scramble their confident affirmations. Beyond an easy play on words, I was also drawn to the icon of the feral⇝ pigeon, a well-known character that gets away with making a living in the margins of urban activity worldwide. It describes a way of operating that is wilfully wild or street-wild, as opposed to romantically wild (like the wolf). In terms of trade, what this approach amounts to is not some kind of heroic or folkloric revival of artisan trade practices. Instead, it is a diy⇝ endeavour with a scavenger's attitude to infrastructure that is inquisitive,

1. feraltrade.org.

⇝

encounter-based, opportunistic, and boundary-disregarding.

I am also aware of the more troubled connotations of the term. Being feral⇝ is normally a status conferred from outside with a mixture of description and emotion. While its objective meaning is the gone-wild descendants of formerly domesticated creatures, it is also used as an expression of annoyance or dislike. Its characteristics include being invasive, causing disruption, being undisciplined⇝ and disorderly, 'wandering all over the place' as literary and historical scholar Alexis Harley puts it.[2] By contrast, the *Feral Atlas* project (see this lexicon) does not make judgements of feral⇝ phenomena but considers them in context. In their careful reading, the feral⇝ is not inherently the problem but a descriptive characteristic of the unintended effects of human infrastructure projects, producing entities that thrive outside human control.

Yet it is in this mixed messaging, its ambivalent character, that the feral⇝ gets interesting. Engaged outside its usual stamping ground of the nature/culture divide, I am intrigued by its potential to run interference in that other super-naturalized domain of business↦. As a category that 'puts pressure on the idea of nature', in Harley's words, it applies stubborn resistance to a naturalized business↦ ideology with its jungle laws of expedition, competition, and Darwinian survival. At the same time, the feral⇝ also signals a departure from the weighty imperatives in social and ethical business↦ to always be 'good' or do 'right'. That an individual enterprise or even a sector could be sustainable or responsible in an unsustainable, irresponsible system is 'implausible', as

2. Alexis Harley, 'Outlaws and Familiars', *Unlikely: Journal of the Creative Arts* 7 (2021), available at unlikely.net.au/issue-1/about-43.

ecological thinkers and action research business↦ scholars Judi Marshall, Peter Reason and Gillian Coleman underline.[3] We need some more down-to-earth assignments.

In this, I consider the feral⇝ as an opportune agent for our times: a scrappy role model, perhaps one-legged, poised to seek out the chinks in seeming impermeable yet arguably plentiful systems. An exemplar for living and working in the cracks—being wild amongst, not wild apart—with a management style that might be well suited for the troubled planetary relations in which we find ourselves. To further investigate this potential in company, I am starting up the Feral MBA, a radically reoriented training course in business↦ for artists and others. Its founding intention is to enter and explore the murky territory of business↦ in oblique, hopeful, hands-on and unstable ways, with the feral⇝ as its emblem.

3. Judi Marshall, Gill Coleman and Peter Reason, *Leadership for Sustainability: An Action Research Approach* (London: Routledge, 2011).

transdisciplinary

Feral Atlas (Lili Carr & Feifei Zhou)

The more-than-human Anthropocene is multiscalar, patchy, and overlapping. Its landscapes, its histories, its ecologies do not line up neatly. To study these more-than human worlds in active formation, *Feral Atlas* argues the need for multiple, multiperspectival accounts that are *transdisciplinary* in approach, method, and form.

Centuries of disciplinary precedent have siloed knowledge-making practices, making it difficult for scholars to study entangled Anthropocene histories that bring attention to humans and nonhumans at the same time. The following caricature is over-the-top, and yet there is a grain of truth in it: Humanists are severed heads floating in the stratosphere of philosophy, while scientists are toes grubbing in empirical dirt. Even in turning towards the concrete, humanists too often stop at an abstract discussion of 'materiality' before they even get to the material itself. Natural scientists ignore such discussions—but to their peril; uninformed by humanist scholarship on politics, history, and culture, scientists too often grab simplistic and misleading paradigms for measuring humanity. None of these habits allow much in the way of conversation. Without this conversation, the false dichotomy of subservient Nature and mastering Culture continues to be affirmed.

Feral Atlas argues that bringing theoretical studies and field-based practices into dialogue—often across lines of mutual unintelligibility and difference—is essential for studying the Anthropocene. *Feral Atlas* contributors describe feral⇝ ecologies based on firsthand observation and assessment (including archival materials) each according to their practice. They are biologists, historians, anthropologists, geographers, climate scientists, artists, poets, and writers; their witnessing comes in various forms, from poetry and natural history to the painting of an Aboriginal artist and the memoir of a British professor. Sometimes, several reports follow the activities of a particular feral⇝ entity, revealing moments of both accord and disconnect. Just as with Anthropocene landscapes, Anthropocene knowledge does not line up neatly either.

During the symposium Making Matters: Collective Material Practices in Critical Times, we (Feral Atlas members Feifei Zhou and Lili Carr) conducted a workshop↦ in noticing feral⇝ effects in the area where you live. The workshop↦ took place online and therefore each participant, all coming from different disciplinary backgrounds and based in their respective homes across Europe, observed and recorded feral⇝ effects around them, each according to their practices. Sharing firsthand observations formed the basis for a rich discussion during the workshop↦. A selection of recordings is reproduced overleaf.

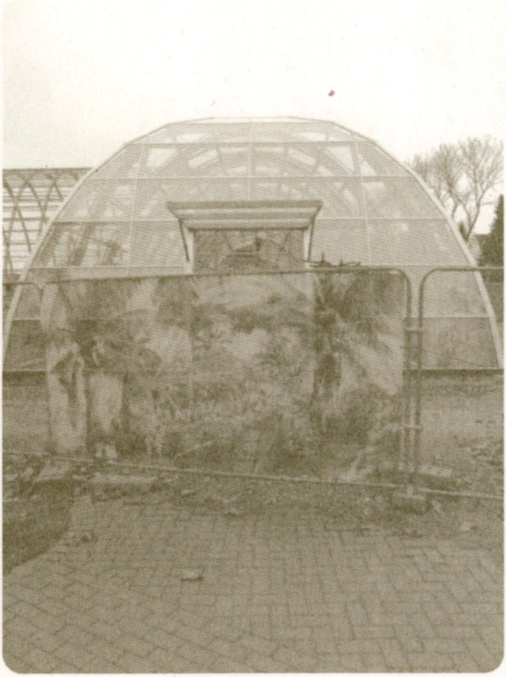

Ann-Katrin Günzel, Cologne. A botanical greenhouse under renovation. Global transport and trade of plants and soils since the early eighteenth century has led to the spread of non-native plant species, pests and disease, many of which have caused world-ripping feral⇝ effects.

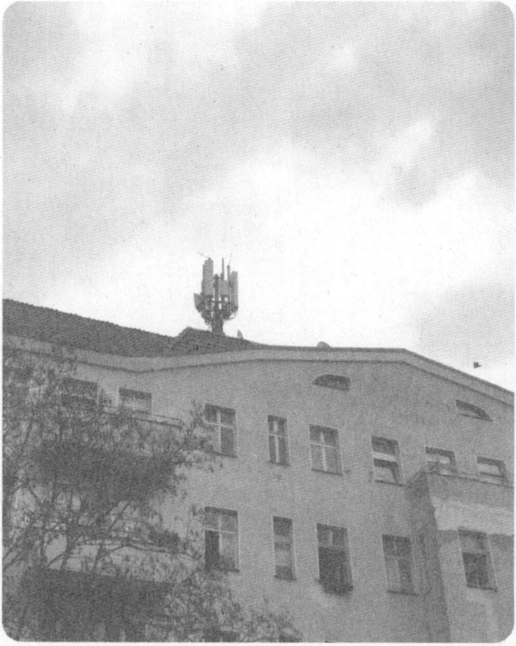

Kate Donovan, Berlin. A Detektor (by Martin Howse and Shintaro Myazaki) detects a cacophony of EM radiation beyond human audible range. There is some indication (yet still limited research) that EM radiation generated by human-made telecommunications infrastructures (such as transmission towers, antennas and cables) has a detrimental effect on certain bird, insect, fish, crustacean, reptilian, mammal and plant life, while the physical infrastructures themselves have been observed to affect migration patterns. ▲ ▶

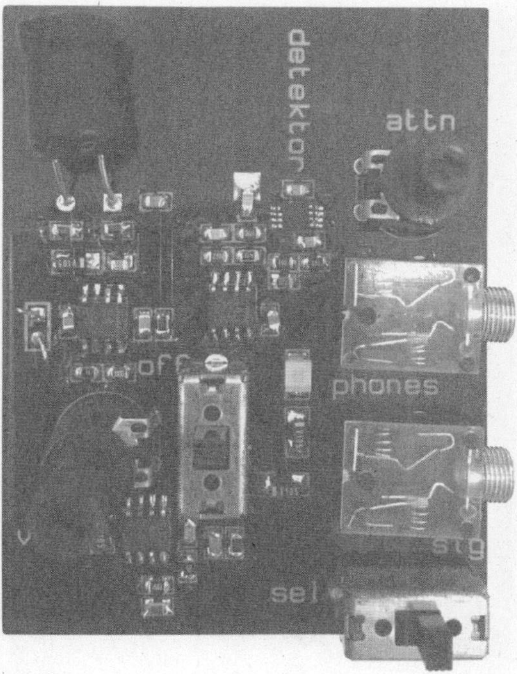
detektor
attn
off
phones
sig
sel

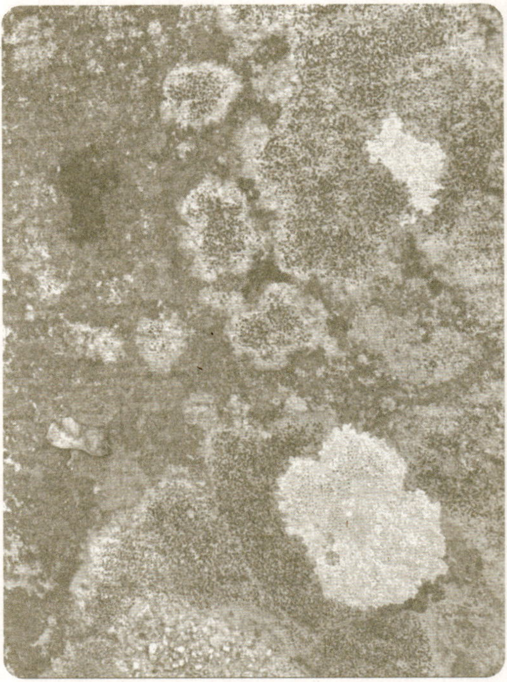

Anthea Oestreicher, Karlsruhe. An increase in the variety of lichens observed during the Covid-19 pandemic indicates a fall in particulate air pollution levels. ▲ ▶

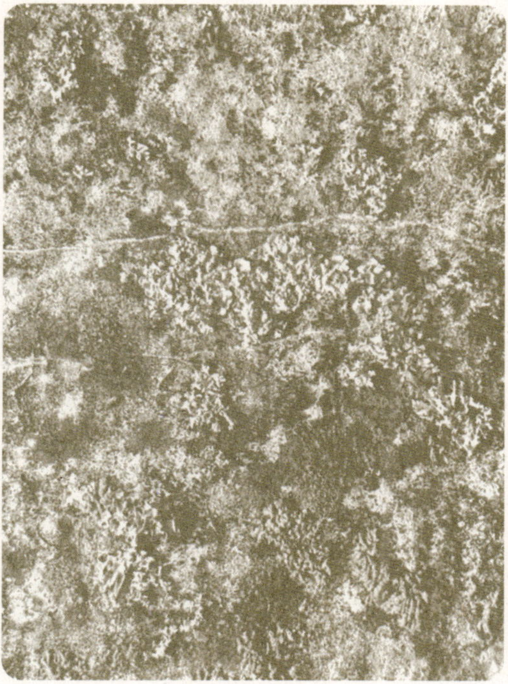

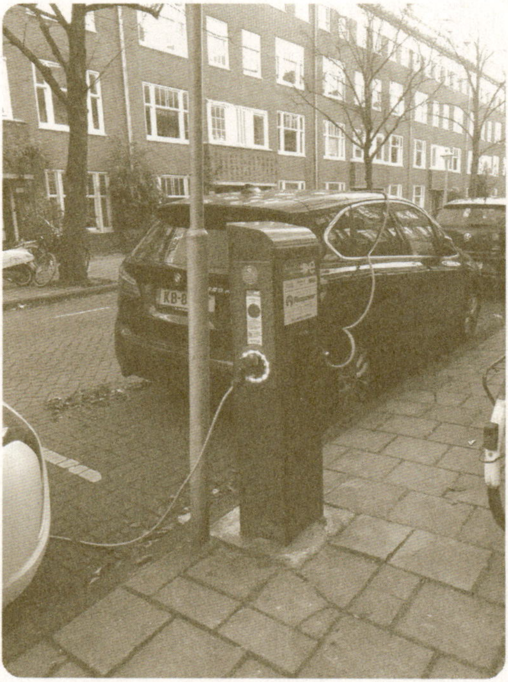

Amsterdam. The installation of EV charging infrastructure underground causes ground temperatures to rise, encouraging the proliferation of potentially harmful pathogens in municipal water pipes. ▲ ▶

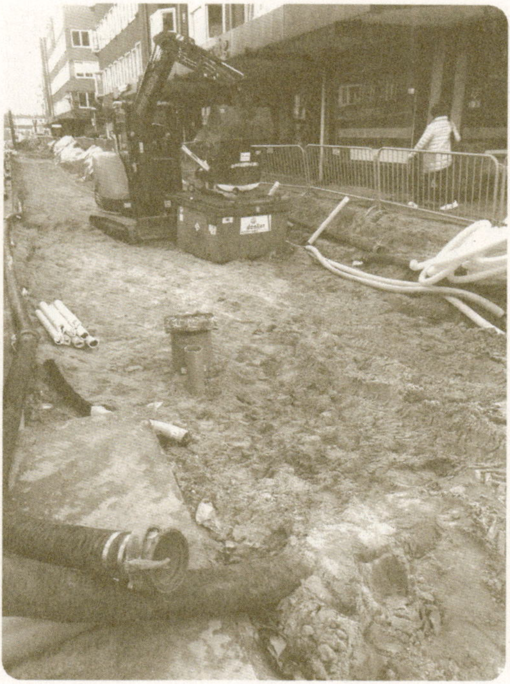

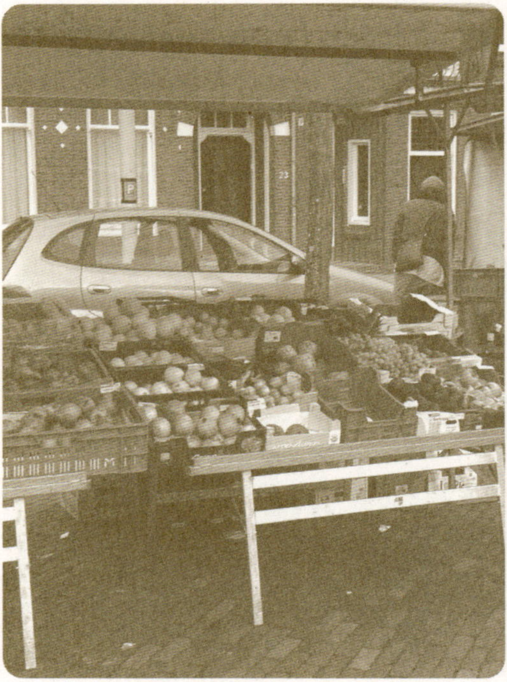

Katharina Wilting, Copenhagen. Tropical fruits are sold at a street market in winter. The pallets on which they are transported overseas harbour non-native insects which, when introduced to new habits, can flourish and spread.

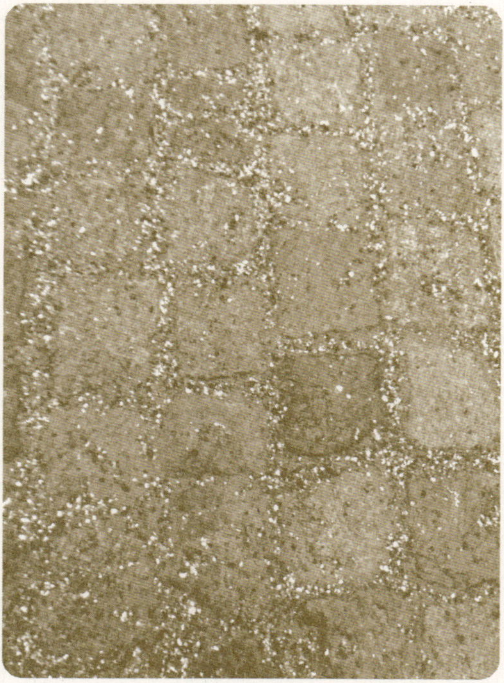

Zeenath Hasan, Copenhagen. The chemicals in rock salt spread to prevent the formation of road-ice is dissolved by run-off and leaks into the groundwater.

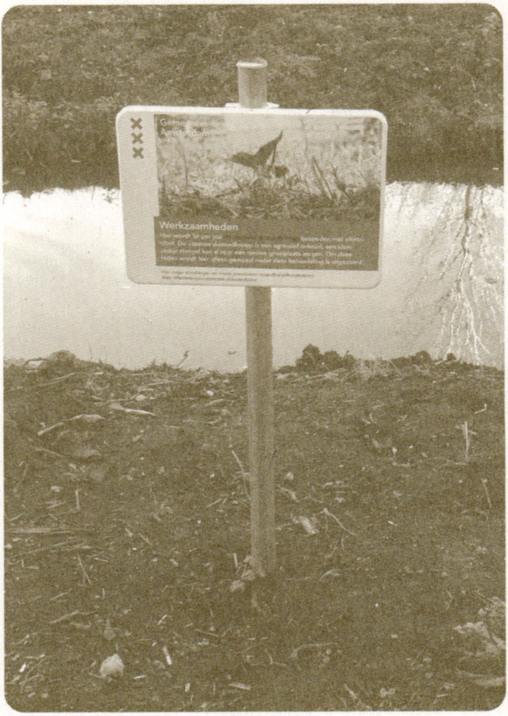

Amsterdam. A marker indicates that on this site treatment for the eradication of Japanese knotweed is taking place. Japanese knotweed was introduced to the Netherlands as an ornamental plant in the mid-nineteenth century and spread through Europe's botanical gardens. It's known to break through concrete and destroy roads, foundations, and in the Netherlands dykes.

underground

Janneke Wesseling

In a lecture delivered on 20 March 1961, entitled 'Where do we go from here?', Marcel Duchamp predicted that in the future artists 'will go *underground*.'[1] The reason for this, Duchamp claimed, was that art had 'degenerated', as he called it, into a gigantic artistic production that was determined by supply and demand, rendering the art object into a commodity. This in turn had led to a dilution of artistic values and to the dominance of mediocre art. The response of serious artists to this deterioration of art would be, according to Duchamp, 'an ascetic revolution'.

A short elaboration on the notion of underground, as used by Duchamp, is needed here. Two years after Duchamp's lecture, the experimental film *Flaming Creatures* by American film director Jack Smith was first shown (at the Bleecker Street Cinema, on 29 April 1963). This film, which celebrates free and queer sex, marks the beginnings of the Underground Film Movement in New York, which would include artists and filmmakers such as Andy Warhol and the Kuchar brothers. The Underground Film Movement also developed ties with hippie subculture and is associated with the writers of the Beat Generation.[2]

This is not the notion of underground that Duchamp was referring to. In my view, Duchamp talked about going underground in the sense of a secret operation, of disappearing from public view as an artist and going into hiding beneath the surface of the earth. How he dealt with his own last work, *Étant donnés*, over a long period of some twenty years between 1946–1966 during which he was believed to have stopped making art altogether, can be seen as an example. Underground is used here in a more literal sense, and

1. invisiblecity.uarts.edu/where-do-we-go-from-here, accessed 3 May 2021.
2. Such as Jack Kerouac, Allen Ginsberg and William S. Burroughs. Another example of underground culture is punk culture in the 1980s.

that is how I will refer to the notion of underground in this essay. An early example is the case of Dick Raaijmakers (1930–2013), Dutch avantgarde composer, performance artist, and founder of Dutch electronic music in the 1950s. Raaijmakers once described his way of operating as follows:

> I dig burrows underground and every once in a while, I stick my head above ground: hello, here I am! When I receive a blow on the head I go back into hiding, I dig further, and try again at a later point in time. If I am hit on the head once again, I withdraw again into the dark. Until finally somebody appreciates the value of my work and is willing to collaborate with me. That is the moment I can show something above ground.[3]

Going underground enables the artist to retain a certain freedom in carrying out the artistic practice, by severing ties with art institutions⊕→ and remaining at a distance from the marketing system and from neoliberalist cultural policies.

We find ourselves right in the middle of, in Duchamp's terminology, such an 'ascetic revolution'—although this revolution differs from what Duchamp had in mind, the main difference being that 'the great artist of tomorrow', as Duchamp called him (for Duchamp, the artist is male), is largely absent as an individual. Forms of collectivity and collaboration are at the heart of the present ascetic revolution. Artists

3. In a conversation with his friend and colleague Frans de Ruiter (n.d.).

join forces in collective endeavours and projects on a global scale. In doing so, values that traditionally have determined artistic production in the Western world are abolished, such as personal signature, copyright, property, marketing values, fame, and the individuality of the artistic genius. All of the contributors to the Making Matters symposia and to the present book testify to this ascetic revolution. These artists have gone underground by withdrawing from the traditional platforms⇛ of the Western art world and by rendering themselves and their art to a certain extent invisible, that is, invisible as manifestations of individual art practices.[4]

Going underground might sound like a defeat to some readers, but in fact it means quite the opposite.[5] Going underground is *not* an exodus from the art world and society, it is not a flight, a retreat, or a search for refuge. Going underground, in the sense it is used here, entails a refusal of solitary gestures⇢, and it aims for a re-grouping, a re-assembling, a re-connecting of forces, a re-configuring of social bonds. It is about *re*affirming relations, rather than about cutting ties. It is, therefore, a political act.

Politics of Withdrawal (2020), a volume edited by the Dutch cultural theorists Joost de Blooijs and Pepita Hesselberth, addresses the meaning of withdrawal as a political act.[6] In their introduction, 'Toward a Politics of

4. Of course, many artists continue to operate 'above ground'; although the Covid-19 pandemic has delivered a serious blow to international art fairs and commercial galleries, the market mechanisms of the art world seem to be still firmly in place.

5. At least, in the meaning intended here. Of course, some artists might go underground as an act of refusal and disappearance, as an act of quitting; think for example of the artist as mystic or shaman.

6. Pepita Hesselberth and Joost de Bloois, ed., *Politics of Withdrawal: Media, Arts, Theory* (Lanham, MD etc. : Rowman & Littlefield, 2020).

Withdrawal?', De Blooijs and Hesselberth suggest that withdrawal

> is not a retreat from actuality per se, but from certain of its aspects: from our present-day 'always-on' culture, from surveillance capitalism, from neo-liberal management, and so on. ... The gesture⇢ interrupts the forward motion of late-capitalism, as withdrawal is not oriented toward the future but rather invested in the possibilities of a different way of life ...[7]

Indeed, underground artists resist the idea of art practice as a form of commercial entrepreneurship aimed at maximum financial profit for the individual entrepreneur, and they refuse to define the value of art as economic value. They distance themselves from neoliberalist policies, and from Western post-colonial dominance in the fields of art and culture. The ways in which this happens are manifold and may include practices that adapt late-capitalist technologies and systems (such as business↦ models, the logistic⇝ of the warehouse and of digital distribution↣ systems) to critically reflect on and inverse capitalist value systems. The distancing can equally happen as overt political activism or as a silent, un-outspoken way of operating that may lead to a certain degree of invisibility. Taking a distance therefore does not involve a negative act of withdrawal in the sense of refusal or seclusion (cf. Henry David Thoreau in *Walden*). Instead, it is a reconnecting that may take the shape of embeddedness⇢, of communality or radical inclusivity.

7. Ibid., p. 13.

The critique of global capitalist logistic⇝ structures and the questioning of the place of technology in culture does not necessarily prevent a positive embracing of new technologies. In fact, a precondition for going underground seems to be an active engagement with the Internet and with technical infrastructures, enabling an opening up of new zones of global collaboration and political action. Thinking with, and through, digital technology and its role in the co-existence of humans and other-than-humans is precisely one of the focal points of the new underground art.

undisciplined

Femke Snelting

⤳

To define the term *undisciplined* is probably a contradiction.[1]

Undisciplined practice is too busy with proliferating sensibilities, issues, demands, requests, complaints, entanglements, methods, and questions to bother with the inherent etiquette of disciplinarity. It insists on a mode of thinking and making that is situated and ad-hoc. It is anti-solutionist and motivated by the need for rigorous uncalibration and disobedient action research.[2]

Undisciplined practitioners often operate collectively. They do not count on validated forms of expertise before interrogating existing ways of doing, and start experimenting with how to do things otherwise, right away. They smuggle techniques from one domain to another, contaminate ethnographic descriptions with accounts of software, mix poetics with abnormal visual renders and blur theoretical dissertations with case-stories.

Undisciplined practice materializes in the use of made-up terminology and uncommon writing, but also in a hands-on engagement with tools, merging high and low tech, learning on the go: active archives, poetic algorithms, body and software, books with an attitude, cqrrelations,[3] counter cartographies, situated

1. See for example how design educators Anja Kaiser and Rebecca Stephany avoid defining the term in order to make it useful: 'Undisciplinarity is not a(nother) binary branding exercise ... we work with undisciplinarity as a feminist unpacking of the discipline of graphic design itself.' *Glossary of Undisciplined Design*, ed. Anja Kaiser and Rebecca Stephany (Leipzig: Spector Books, 2021), p. 4.
2. Possible Bodies, 'Polyedric Research Methods', in *Volumetric Regimes: Material Cultures of Quantified Presence*, ed. Jara Rocha and Femke Snelting (Open Humanities Press, in press).
3. 'Cqrrelation is poetry to the statistician. It is science to the dissident. It is detox to the data-addict.' Cqrrelations, work session (Brussels, Constant, 2015).

publishing, e-traces, ex-titutional networks, interstitial work, libre graphics, performative protocols, relearning, discursive infrastructures, hackable devices.[4]

4. This list of invented practices may read as a manifesto, but actually describes the daily activities of the Brussels-based association for art and media, Constant. Their publications, workshops↦, methods, and other interventions are an ongoing attempt to imagine what technological practice could be when oriented by intersectional feminisms, collective authorship and Free, Libre and Open Source software. This work is developed in collaboration with maker-researchers moving in and out of various (un)disciplines: artists, activists, designers, passers-by, theorists, programmers, fans, filmmakers, writers. *About Constant*, constantvzw.org/site/-About-Constant-7-.html, accessed 27 April 2021.

index

contributors

Authors and Editors

Aliens in Green (Bureau d'études, Ewen Chardronnet, Mary Maggic, Julien Maudet, Špela Petrič) is an investigative laboratory and tactical theatre group combating the alien agents of anthropogenic xeno-power. The lab implements intermedia processes that connect open science, DIY bio practices, dietetics, speculative narration, serious games, cultural intelligence and science fiction to generate critical discourse and interventions in the public sphere. One may understand Aliens in Green lab as both a symmetrical and antagonist entity to the 'Men in Black'. They act as discursive agents dealing with human relations and life forms of a third type. But unlike 'Men in Black' who operate secretly and erase people's memories, Aliens in Green act openly and tactically, allowing earthlings to identify the numerous collusions between capitalist and xeno-political forces.
aliensingreen.eu

Lili Carr (born 1986) is an architect who studied at the Architectural Association in London. Her work explores how alternative models of architecture practice can encourage attention to the non-designed ecological effects of designed spatial and material transformation. Recent exhibitions include: 'Vegetation Under Power' (co-curated with Maya Errázuriz, Shaiwanti Gupta, Elizabeth Hong, Pierre Klein, Elisabetta Rattalino, Shivani Shedde & Nancy Valladares), Bauhaus Dessau Foundation, Dessau, 2021; 'Free School of Architecture' (co-curated with Karina Andreeva, Elisha Cohen & Tessa Forde), WUHO Gallery, Los Angeles, 2018. Recent contributed

articles include 'Infrastructures in the More-Than-Human Anthropocene' (co-authored with Feifei Zhou and Anna L.Tsing) in *KERB Journal of Landscape Architecture* 28: Decentre (2020). Carr lives and works between the UK and Amsterdam.
lilicarr.net

Florian Cramer (born 1969, DE) is a reader in autonomous art and design practices at Willem de Kooning Academy and Piet Zwart Institute, Rotterdam, the Netherlands. His work focuses on multidisciplinary, self-organized, communal art practices. He is a contributor to artist-run initiatives including the Voluntary Fire Brigade of the Apocalypse, Radio WORM and BananSkole. Recent publications include *Artistic Research: Dead on Arrival?* Research practices of self-organized collectives versus managerial visions of artistic research (in: *The Postresearch Condition*, 2021) and *Pattern Discrimination* (2018) (co-edited with Clemens Apprich, Wendy Hui Kyong Chun and Hito Steyerl). Cramer lives and works in Rotterdam.
floriancramer.nl

Display Distribute is a thematic inquiry, distribution service, now and again exhibition space and sometimes shop founded in Kowloon in 2013. Seeping via the capricious circulation patterns of low-end globalization into other subaltern networks and grammars, recent activities include manoeuvring and reading with the Black Book Assembly, experimental infrastructure LIGHT LOGISTICS, poetic research and archival unit Shanzhai Lyric, the readers' digest publication CATALOGUE and a peripatetic radio programme of hidden feminist narratives known as Widow Radio Ching.
displaydistribute.com

Feral Atlas (published 2020, Stanford University Press) is a collective work of more than a hundred scientists, humanists, and artists, united in examining the non-designed effects of human-made infrastructures. Feral Atlas is curated and edited by anthropologist Anna L. Tsing, visual anthropologist Jennifer Deger, environmental anthropologist Alder Keleman Saxena and architect Feifei Zhou. The project is developed in collaboration with architect Lili Carr and an international network of makers, designers, artists, editors, and coders. Recent exhibitions include: 'Vienna Biennial for Change 2021', MAK–Museum of Applied Arts, Vienna, 2021; 'The World Around Summit 2021', The Guggenheim, New York, 2021; Sharjah Architecture Triennial, Sharjah, 2019–2020; Istanbul Biennial, Istanbul, 2019.
feralatlas.org

Baruch Gottlieb (born 1966, CA) is an artist, curator, and writer specialized in data epistemology and techno-aesthetics. Trained as a filmmaker at Concordia University Montreal, he has a doctorate from the University of Arts Berlin where he teaches and runs the Research Institute for Technical Aesthetics (RITA). He curates and contributes to the programme at West Den Haag and is founder, with Steffi Winkler, of flusser.club, an organization dedicated to the work of Vilém Flusser. He is a core member of the Telekommunisten and disnovation.org artist collectives. His latest book is *Digital Materialism* (Emerald, 2018).

Anja Groten (born 1983, DE) is a designer, researcher, and educator based in Amsterdam. Investigating collectivity in practice, her work revolves around the cross-section of digital and physical media, design and art education and her involvement in different interdisciplinary groups. In 2013 she co-founded the initiative Hackers & Designers, in an attempt to break down the barriers between the two fields by enforcing a common vocabulary through education, hacks, and collaboration. Anja is a PhD candidate at PhDArts, and the consortium Bridging Art, Design and Technology through Critical Making. In 2019 she became course director of the design department at the Sandberg Instituut Amsterdam (Master of the Gerrit Rietveld Academie).

anjagroten.info

Akiem Helmling (born 1971, DE) is partner and co-founder of the type-collective Underware (underware.nl/) and co-founder of the contemporary art centre West Den Haag. He studied graphic design at the FH Mannheim and type design at the Royal Academy of Art, The Hague. His interest lies in connecting people and challenging them to think through art. Helmling is curator of Alphabetum, the space dedicated to letters, writing, and philosophy at West. Recent projects include: 'L'écriture avant la lettre' (2022): 'Writing Writing' (2020), 'Free Emoji' (2020), 'Laws of Form' (2019) and 'From Typography to Grammatograhy' (2019).

Elaine W. Ho works between the realms of time-based art, language, and urban practice. She is the founder of artist-run project space HomeShop (Beijing, 2008–13) and continues to ask questions about the sociopolitics of syntax, more recently via ongoing collaborations with Amy Suo Wu, Display Distribute, and • • PROPAGANDA DEPARTMENT. Their work has been presented on a boat named Eleonore, docked along the Danube River (Linz, 2016), at the Singapore Biennial (2019), Hamburger Bahnhof (2017), Seoul Mediacity Biennale (2017),

Power Station of Art (2016), Guangdong Times Museum (2021/2015), and on various street corners, among other places.
indexofho.net

Thalia Hoffman (born 1979, DE) is an visual artist working in film, performance and public interventions in the area she lives in, east of the Mediterranean. Studied at ACPA, PhDArts programme at Leiden University, and currently teaches at the University of Haifa and the KABK. Her work strives to be involved in its surroundings and engage people to look, listen, and feel their socio-political landscape with attention. Recent exhibitions include: 'Art has a Smell', The Farm Gallery, Holon, Israel (2021); Experiments in Cinema, Albuquerque (NM), (2020); Striving for Touch performance festival, Jaffa (2020). Thalia Hoffman, lives and works in Jaffa–Tel Aviv.

Jatiwangi art Factory (2005) is a community that embraces contemporary arts and cultural practices as part of the local life discourse in a rural area. Their manifold activities, always involving the local public, include a video festival, a music festival, a residency programme, a discussion series, and a TV and radio station. At the beginning of the twentieth century, its clay industry made Jatiwangi the biggest roof tile producing region in Southeast Asia. A hundred years later, in 2005, using the same clay, JaF encouraged the people of Jatiwangi to create a collective awareness and identity for their region through arts and cultural activity. In doing so, JaF tries to cultivate clay with more dignity and to raise the collective happiness of the community.
jatiwangiartfactory.tumblr.com

Eleni Kamma (born 1973, GR) is an artist and researcher. She holds a doctorate in artistic research from PhDArts. Kamma's practice circulates from her as an individual artist (through drawings and objects) to dialogic collaborations (films, performative events, journals) and back again, by writing about it and further developing this practice with others. Recent solo exhibitions include: 'Casting Call: The Collector of Proverbs, The Animal, The Fool, The Selfie-Junkie, The Innocent, The Child, The Drunk, The...', West Den Haag, 2021; 'Casting Call: So, You Think About Abstraction the Last Minutes Before You Die?', SPACE, Liege, 2021. Kamma lives and works in Brussels and Maastricht.
elenikamma.com

Frans-Willem Korsten (born 1959, NL) holds the chair 'Literature and Society' by special appointment at the Erasmus School of Philosophy, and works at the Leiden University Centre for the Arts in Society. He has published monographs on the Dutch baroque, theatricality and sovereignty and has written about the relation between literature, art, capitalism, and law. He participates in the NWO funded programme 'Playing Politics: Media Platforms, Making Worlds', and most recently published *Art as an Interface of Law and Justice: Affirmation, Disturbance, Disruption*; (2021).

Klaas Kuitenbrouwer (born 1964, NL) is a researcher, curator, educator. He studied History at the University of Utrecht. Currently he is Senior Researcher at Het Nieuwe Instituut in Rotterdam, where he initiated the Zoöp project. He works at the crossroads of culture, technology and ecology, with a special focus on the intersection of knowledge practices. Recent exhibitions include 'Neuhaus—Temporary Academy for more-than-human Knowledge', Het Nieuwe Instituut. Rotterdam, 2019, 'Gardening Mars', Het Nieuwe Instituut, Rotterdam, 2018. He co-edited *Vertical Atlas* (2022) together with Nyanjala Nyabola, Mi You, Amal Khalaf, Leonardo Dellanoce, and Arthur Steiner. He lives and mostly works in Amsterdam.

Pia Louwerens (born 1990, NL) is an artistic researcher, artist and writer. She has completed a post-master and fellowship programme at a.pass (advanced performance and scenography studies), Brussels. In 2021 she self-published her book *I'm Not Sad, The World Is Sad*, an autotheoretical, semi-fictional account of the increasingly paranoid relationship between an artistic researcher and the art institution where she is 'embedded'. Next to her artistic practice Louwerens has written texts for *De Witte Raaf*, *Metropolis M*, *Tubelight* and *Het Parool*. Pia Louwerens lives and works in Brussels.

Lilia Mestre (born 1968, PT) is a performing artist and researcher working mainly in collaboration with other artists. She is currently the artistic coordinator of a.pass (Advanced Performance and Scenography Studies). Mestre works with assemblages, scores, inter-subjective set ups and other chance-induced processes as an artist, curator, dramaturge and co-learner. She is interested in forms of sociability created by artistic practice and she composes with semiotic agencies to explore these in her work. Mestre works and lives in Brussels.

Dani Ploeger (NL) is an artist and cultural theorist who explores situations of conflict and crisis on the fringes of the world of high-tech consumerism. He is currently a Research Fellow at The Royal Central School of Speech and Drama, University of London,

and a Fellow at V2_Lab for the Unstable Media in Rotterdam. His artwork has been exhibited in museums, galleries and biennales worldwide, including ZKM Centre for Art and Media Karlsruhe, Venice Architecture Biennale and the Nairobi National Museum. He is the author of *Deserted Devices and Wasted Fences: Everyday Technologies in Extreme Circumstances* (2021).
daniploeger.org

Kate Rich (born 1968, AU) is an artist, trader and feral economist. She is currently undertaking PhD research into the 'Feral MBA', a radically different training course in business for artists and others, at the University of the West of England. She is part of the finance team at Bristol's Cube Microplex and co-founder of the Institute of Experiments with Business (Ibex) with transnational network FoAM. Other active business interests include: Cube-Cola, co-manufactured with Kayle Brandon (since 2004); and Feral Trade, a sole trader grocery business (since 2003). Rich lives and works in Bristol UK and temporarily in Tasmania, Australia.

Femke Snelting (born 1969, NL) develops projects at the intersection of design, feminisms, and Free Software. With Seda Guerses, Miriyam Aouragh and Helen Pritchard, she runs The Institute for Technology in the Public Interest. With Jara Rocha, she studies material cultures of quantified presence in the disobedient action research project Volumetric Regimes and computational imaginations of rock formations with the Underground Division (Helen Pritchard, Jara Rocha). Femke supports artistic research at PhDArts (Leiden), MERIAN (Maastricht) and a.pass (Brussels). She occasionally teaches at XPUB (Rotterdam).
snelting.domainepublic.net

Marie-José Sondeijker is co-founder and director of West Den Haag. West presents contemporary art in the former American embassy in the heart of the The Hague museum district. The art institute focuses on the most relevant international developments in the field of visual arts. As curator she made exhibitions with Gregor Schneider, Tehching Hsieh, Carol Rama, Douglas Park, Gustav Metzger, and dozens of others. She has also worked with authors, curators, musicians and filmmakers from various countries.

Olu Taiwo is a senior lecturer at the University of Winchester. Olu teaches in Street Arts, Visual Development and Contemporary Performance in a combination of real and virtual formats. He has a background in Fine Art, Street Dance, African percussion, physical theatre and the martial arts. He has performed in national and international contexts pioneering concepts surrounding practice as research. This includes how practice as a research strategy can explore the nature of performance and the relationships between 'effort', 'performance', and 'performative actions' as they occur in different arenas. Consequently, his aim is—through the use of practice—to propagate twenty-first century issues concerning the interaction between the body, identity, audience, street and technology in an age of Globalization. His interests include: Practice as Research, Visual design, Movement, Theatre, Street Arts, New technology, Trans-cultural studies, Geometry, Philosophy and Religious studies.

Janneke Wesseling (born 1955, NL) is an art historian and art critic. She obtained a doctoral degree at Leiden University with a dissertation on contemporary art and reception aesthetics. Wesseling is Professor in the Practice and Theory of Research in the Visual

Arts, Faculty of Humanities, Leiden University (NL). She is director of PhDArts, international doctorate programme in visual art and design, at the Academy of Creative and Performing Arts (ACPA) of Leiden University, and head of the Research Group in Art Theory & Practice at the University of the Arts, The Hague. Wesseling writes as an art critic for the Dutch daily *NRC Handelsblad*.

Feifei Zhou (born 1992, CN) is a spatial and visual designer and an Associate Lecturer for MA and BA Architecture at Central Saint Martins, University of the Arts, London. Her work explores spatial, cultural, and ecological impacts of the industrialized built and natural environment. Recent publications include: *Feral Atlas: The More-Than-Human Anthropocene* (co-edited with Anna L.Tsing, Jennifer Deger, Alder Keleman Saxena) (2020). Recently contributed articles include 'Noticing the Anthropocene' in *Inflection Vol. 08 Presence: Journal of the Melbourne School of Design* (2021); 'Root Seeker' in *e-flux* (2021); 'Architects Draw the Anthropocene' (co-authored with Lili Carr and Anna L.Tsing) in *Perspecta 53: Onus Yale School of Architecture Journal* (2020). Zhou lives and works in London.
feifeizhou.com

Z. Blace (born 1976, SFR Yugoslavia) is an anti-disciplinary artivist, cultural worker, and queer instigator, who studied at Fine Arts Academies in Zagreb and Sarajevo, also with Keiko Sei & Vasulkas (FaVU Brno) and Nan Hoover (Summer Academy Salzburg). Ze was media/design researcher at Jan van Eyck Academie and doctoral candidate in PhDArts at Royal Academy of Art, The Hague. Ze is (in+) consistently working (in-)between fields of contemporary culture and arts, digital technology and

media, community sports and activism—by cross-pollinating queer/commoning perspectives and embodied experiences with thinking and doing methods across different networks and contexts.
wikidata.org/wiki/Q101768830

Other Contributors

Lucas Evers is trained in fine arts and teaching at Maastricht Academy of Fine Arts and Design and he studied political science at the University of Amsterdam. He worked at De Balie, Centre for Culture and Politics and the Melkweg in Amsterdam, programming cinema, new media, and politics. He is currently Head of Programme of Make at Waag–Technology & Society, where he is actively involved in several projects that concern the interactions between the arts and sciences and contemporary maker culture. He is co-editor of *Open Design Now: Why Design Cannot Remain Exclusive* (opendesignnow.org). Waag operates at the intersection of science, technology and the arts, focusing on technology as an instrument of social change, guided by the values of fairness, openness, and inclusivity. Make researches materials, material practices, as well as the social and ecological meaning and future impact of these materials and processes.

Coordinator of the Project

Emily Huurdeman (born 1985, NL) is a Dutch artist, researcher and educator. As an artist she works with video and performance. Her research revolves around theorizing and practicing essaying as unmethodological method for artistic research. She presented her work at multiple international conferences and has published an academic article on the topic. As a teacher she works at multiple art institutions in the Netherlands. She is the coordinator of the Lectorate Art, Theory & Practice and the NWO/SIA funded research project Making Matters at ACPA Leiden University, both headed by Prof. dr. Janneke Wesseling. She is also the co-initiator of Café Chercher, and art café for unfinished art and research projects.

egahuurdeman.nl

Partner Institutes Research Project

Academy of Creative and Performing Arts / PhDArts
PhDArts, an international doctorate programme in art and design, is a collaboration between Leiden University Academy of Creative and Performing Arts (ACPA) and the Royal Academy of Art (KABK) in The Hague.
phdarts.eu

Het Nieuwe Instituut
Het Nieuwe Instituut hosts exhibitions and debates on architecture, design and digital culture in Rotterdam, the Netherlands, and develops new practices that combine these fields.
hetnieuweinstituut.nl

Waag
Waag Future Lab contributes to the research, design, and development of a sustainable, just society by collectively researching emerging technology and questioning underlying cultural assumptions; by experimenting with and designing alternatives on the basis of public values; by developing an open, fair, and inclusive future together with civil society.
waag.org

West Den Haag
West Den Haag presents contemporary art in a brutalist Breuer building, offers artists space to develop new work and, through a broad dialogue, places it in a social context.
westdenhaag.nl

Willem de Kooning Academy
In its research programme Autonomous Practices, Willem de Kooning Academy (WdKA), an art and

design school in Rotterdam, investigates new concepts of autonomy and self-organization in contemporary arts.
wdka.nl

Designers

Anja Groten, Heerko van der Kooij, Juliette Lizotte, Karl Moubarak (Hackers & Designers)
Hackers & Designers is a non-profit initiative organizing activities at the intersection of technology, design and art. By creating shared moments of hands-on learning H&D stimulates collaboration across disciplines, technological literacy, and different levels of expertise. H&D members at the time of this publication are Loes Bogers, André Fincato, Selby Gildemacher, Anja Groten, Heerko van der Kooij, Juliette Lizotte, Karl Moubarak, Christine Kappé, and Pernilla Manjula Philip.
hackersanddesigners.nl

Publisher

Valiz is an independent international publisher, addressing contemporary developments in art, design, architecture, and urban affairs. Their books provide critical reflection and interdisciplinary inspiration in a broad and imaginative way, often establishing a connection between cultural disciplines and socio-economic questions. Valiz is headed by Astrid Vorstermans and Pia Pol, and is based in Amsterdam.
valiz.nl

a note on the design of this publication

As the vocabulary of collective arts is intersecting many fields of knowledge that cannot be easily confined to separate categories, terms also spill over into other definitions and other chapter themes. The design of this publication accommodates non-linear reading, without compromising orientation. That is, cross-references are indicated with seven different kinds of arrows, referring to one of the seven chapter themes. The arrows occur on the chapter introduction pages, next to the respective terms, as well as in the side bar navigation of the respective chapter categories. This allows the reader to quickly sift through the book and find terms in different contexts. In addition, elements in the side bar navigation subtly poke out when indicating the occurrence of a term in the text.

The design of this book is part of an ongoing collective exploration into unusual, non-proprietary, open-source, free and libre publishing tools and workflows. Such tools come with their own quirks and ask us to re-think and re-shuffle design priorities. For instance, when it comes to detail typography—the perfect line break or kerning, we had to make concessions in this publication. Still, by putting into practice different tool-designer scenarios we hope to contribute to a growing community of designers who consider it relevant to rethink their tool-ecologies. Building on the knowledge and practices of many designers and collectives that work with and contribute to open-source approaches to designing on and offline publications,[1] Hackers & Designers' publishing experiments intersect computer programming, art, and design, and involve the building of self-made, hacked, and reappropriated tools and technical infrastructures, which sometimes results in books, such as the one you are holding now.

Following open-source principles, the tool ecosystem that evolved around the design of this publication is documented and published on the H&D website[2] and git repository[3] under the CC4r license,[4] providing the possibility of continuation in other contexts, studying, critiquing, and repurposing.

The tools ecosystem includes: MediaWiki, Jinja templating, Pagedjs for the layout, and Scribus & Gimp for image retouching and cover design.

All typefaces used in this publication are available at 'Badass Libre Fonts By Womxn',[5] a repository of open source and/or libre typefaces composed by Loraine Furter.

1. Collectives that inspire us in our design experiments are Varia, Constant Association for Art and Media, Open Source Publishing, the practices and knowledge deriving from educational contexts such as the student-led interdepartmental initiative PUB at the Sandberg Instituut Amsterdam or XPUB—a master programme of Experimental Publishing at Piet Zwart Institute, the digital and hybrid publishing research groups of the Institute of Network Cultures. Concretely, the technical infrastructure and workflow used to create this publication (wiki-to-pdf) is building on the code repositories of Martino Morandi (Constant Association for Art and Media) developed for the publication 'Infrastructural Interactions' edited by TITiPI (Helen V Pritchard, Femke Snelting) (gitlab.constantvzw.org/titipi/wiki-to-pdf), and Manetta Berends (Varia Collective) developed for the publication *Volumetric Regimes* edited by Possible Bodies (Jara Rocha, Femke Snelting), published under the CC4r license (git.vvvvvaria.org/mb/volumetric-regimes-book).
2. hackersanddesigners.nl/s/Tools.
3. github.com/hackersanddesigners.
4. constantvzw.org/wefts/cc4r.en.html.
5. design-research.be/by-womxn.

Fonts used: Ortica designed by Benedetta Bovani, Authentic Sans designed by by Christina Janus and Desmond Wong, and Combine designed by Julie Patard.

acknowledgements

This book is an outcome of a collaborative research project conducted by five research and art institutions in the Netherlands: Leiden University, Willem de Kooning Academy, Rotterdam, Het Nieuwe Instituut, Waag Society, and West Den Haag. Its point of departure was rather unlikely: the technocratic creative industries research and development agenda of the Netherlands, conceived by a neoliberal government in the 2010s. The government's cultural policy had boiled down to scrapping arts-related research in favour of digital technology research and development (based on a partial misinterpretation of 'creative industries' as Silicon Valley-style start-ups). Funding for contemporary art was cut, too, in favour of programmes for the creative industries. These policies have caused much wilful damage to the art world in the Netherlands over the past fifteen years.

The representatives of these five institutions came together as the Workgroup Making Matters to explore ways of bridging art, design, and technology as an alternative to the paradigm of 'creative industries'.

The research project and the book are financed by the Smart Culture programme of the Dutch Research Council (NWO).

We received a great amount of support from colleagues in our field: Lotte Betting, Loes Bogers, ginger coons, Garnet Hertz, Emily Huurdeman, Janneke van Kersen (NWO), Shailoh Phillips, Rosalien van der Poel, Marielle Verdijk.

We thank Hackers & Designers for their collaboration and the design of the book.

We thank Het Nieuwe Instituut, West Den Haag and Waag for contributing the work and research time of their people.

colophon

Editors
Janneke Wesseling, Florian Cramer

Editorial committee
Florian Cramer, Anja Groten, Klaas Kuitenbrouwer, Pia Louwerens, Marie-José Sondeijker, Janneke Wesseling

Contributors
Aliens in Green, a.pass / Lilia Mestre, Florian Cramer, Display Distribute / Elaine W. Ho, Feral Atlas / Lili Carr & Feifei Zhou, Anja Groten, Thalia Hoffman, Jatiwangi art Factory / Bunga Siagian & Ismal Muntaha, Eleni Kamma, Frans-Willem Korsten, Klaas Kuitenbrouwer, Pia Louwerens, Dani Ploeger, Kate Rich, Femke Snelting, Olu Taiwo, Janneke Wesseling, West / Baruch Gottlieb, West / Akiem Helmling, Z. Blace (zBlace / Z. Blacé)

Design
Hackers & Designers

Partners
Academy of Creative and Performing Arts, Leiden University
Het Nieuwe Instituut, Rotterdam
Waag, Amsterdam
West Den Haag
Willem de Kooning Academy and Piet Zwart Institute, Rotterdam

Copy-editing
Leo Reijnen

Proofreading
Els Brinkman

Index
Elke Stevens

Paper Inside
Holmen TRND, 70 grs 2.0

Paper Cover
Fedrigoni Acquerello, 220 grs

Lithography
Mariska Bijl, Wilco Art Books, Amsterdam

Printing and Binding
Wilco Art Books, Amersfoort

Publisher
Valiz, Amsterdam,
Astrid Vorstermans & Pia Pol
www.valiz.nl

International distribution

- BE/NL/LU: Centraal Boekhuis, centraal.boekhuis.nl
- GB/IE: Central Books, centralbooks.com
- Europe (excl GB/IE)/Asia: Idea Books, ideabooks.nl
- Australia: Perimeter, perimeterdistribution.com
- USA, Canada, Latin-America: D.A.P., artbook.com
- Individual orders: valiz.nl; info@valiz.nl

Support
The Making Matters research, symposium and this publication have been generously supported by the Dutch Research Council (NWO), part of the project 'Bridging art, design and technology through Critical Making' (project number 314-99-203), research programme Smart Culture.

Valiz, Amsterdam 2022
ISBN 978-94-93246-11-9
Printed and bound in the EU